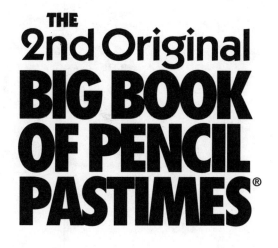

THE
2nd Original
BIG BOOK
OF PENCIL
PASTIMES®

THE
2nd Original
BIG BOOK
OF PENCIL
PASTIMES®

By James F. Minter

Bristol Park Books

First Bristol Park Books edition published in 1993.
New edition published in 2004.

Bristol Park Books, Inc.
450 Raritan Center Parkway
Edison, NJ 08837

Pencil Pastimes is a registered trademark of Bristol Park
Books, Inc.
Bristol Park Books is a registered trademark of Bristol
Park Books, Inc.

Published by arrangement with Hart Associates.

ISBN: 0-88486-323-9

Printed in the United States of America.

Contents

QUIZZES

THREEZIES

CRYPTOGRAMS

PICTURE QUIZZES

ALFABITS

5

The Pipes of Pan

Below you will find 30 expressions, phrases, or names. Each one of these should suggest to you another expression which contains the syllable PAN. For example: *A Central American country* would be PANama.

A score of 16 is good, 20 is excellent, 24 is extraordinary; 28, brilliant.

1. _ _ _ _ _ PAN   Play by James M. Barrie

2. PAN _ _ _ _ _   Temple dedicated to the gods

3. PAN _ _ _ _ _   Wide spectacular view

4. _ _ _ PAN _   Unbridled; threatening; fierce

5. PAN _ _ _ _ _ _ _   Exceptionally wide breeches and trousers

6. _ _ _ PAN   A Chinese boat

7. PAN _ _ _ _   A cure-all

8. PAN _ _ _ _ _ _ _   State of wild uproar

9. PAN _ _ _ _ _ _   To accost on the street and beg

10. PAN _ _ _ _ _ _   Movements unaccompanied by speech

11. PAN _ _ _ _ _   Large gland of the human body

12. PAN _ _ _ _   A tinted cosmetic

13. PAN _ _   Effeminate youth

6

14. _ _ _ _ _ _ _ _ _   _ _ _   Famous novel by Rabelais

    PAN _ _ _ _ _ _ _

15. PAN _ _ _ _   The girl with that evil casket

16. _ _ _ _ _ _ PAN _ _   Don Quixote's attendant

17. PAN _ _ _ _   Swagger; flamboyance

18. PAN _ _   Tibetan teddy bear

19. PAN _ _ _ _ _ _   Laudatory discourse

20. _ PAN _ _ _   Dog with long, drooping ears

21. PAN _ _ _   German armored unit

22. _ _ _ PAN _ _ _   Friend

23. _ _ _ PAN _   Firm; business organization

24. PAN _ _ _   _ _ _ _ _   Famous Mexican bandit

25. _ _ _ PAN   Drum

26. _ _ _ PAN _ _   Of Spanish origin

27. _ _ _ PAN _ _ _   A bell tower

28. _ _ PAN _   To increase in size

29. PAN _   To breathe hard

30. _ _ PAN _ _   Famous naval battle between
                           Christians and Turks (1571)

The Long and Short of it

Each of the 55 terms defined below contains either the word LONG or the word SHORT. For example, "Goodbye" would be *So long*. How many of them can you get?

A score of 35 is good; 40 is excellent; 45 indicates you won't be SHORTchanged.

1. Lack or dearth   _____

2. Possessions or property   _____

3. Hotly-debated 1977 rock song by Randy Newman   _____

4. Dessert of pastry, fruit and whipped cream   _____

5. Ubiquitous police and peace-keeping officers; ultimate retribution   _____

6. Understaffed, with too few assistants   _____

7. American poet ("The Song of Hiawatha")   _____

8. Baseball infield position   _____

9. Character in *Treasure Island*   _____

10. Existing only briefly   _____

11. Popular World War I song   _____

12. Literary form invented by American authors   _____

13. Little Richard song later recorded by the Beatles   _____

14. Chef in a fast-food diner   _____

15. Distance east or west of Greenwich   _____

16. Summertime wear named after an island resort   _____

17. Georgia doctor, first to use ether _____

18. Type of radio favored by "ham" operators _____

19. Cornelius Ryan World War II novel, made into 1962 film _____

20. Faults; limitations _____

21. Louisiana demagogue _____

22. Breathless; lacking lung power _____

23. Extend the duration of _____

24. To relate concisely; to summarize _____

25. Propaganda song sung by Nazis in *Cabaret* _____

26. A native of Milan _____

27. Electrical malfunction _____

28. Infamous Northern Ireland detention camp for political prisoners _____

29. Fat used in pastry-making _____

30. A great risk or unlikely winner _____

31. Type of men's underwear named after horsemen _____

32. Well-known watch manufacturer _____

33. Cut of meat used in "soul food" _____

34. Weapon used in archery _____

35. Stenography _____

36. Very late Beatles song _____

37. Miguel Pinero play and film set in prison _____

38. Slang term for classical music _____

39. Easier way or less-lengthy way _____

39. Easier way or less-lengthy way _____

40. Eugene O'Neill's masterpiece _____

41. Defeat easily and quickly _____

42. Stevedore _____

43. Myopic; without regard to future consequences _____

44. An eighth of a mile _____

45. A starchy Southern food; an American folk song _____

46. A spider _____

47. Inequity; disadvantage _____

48. A type of Chinese tea _____

49. Quick drink _____

50. Great life span _____

51. Bless them all _____

52. Canal in Bangkok _____

53. Mary Martin song _____

54. Temporary loan or investment _____

55. Eventually; later on _____

Place Names

All of the persons described below have one thing in common: each bears a name that contains the name of a city, state, or country. For example, "Noted American playwright" would be TENNESSEE Williams. How many of them can you locate?

A score of 6 is okay; 7 is good; and 11 is really going places.

1. American popular songwriter ("God Bless America")   ————————————

2. The first child born of Colonial parents in the New World   ————————————

3. Depression-era nightclub comedienne, known for the saying, "Hello, suckers."   ————————————

4. American author (*Real Lace, Our Crowd*)   ————————————

5. American writer (*Call of the Wild*)   ————————————

6. Ashley Wilkes' sister in *Gone with the Wind*   ————————————

7. Big gambler in *Guys and Dolls*   ————————————

8. American woman painter (1887-), often uses Southwestern motifs   ————————————

9. French author (*Thais*)   ————————————

10. American sculptor, best-known for "LOVE" statue   ————————————

11. Name by which plainsman William F. Cody is better known   ————————————

12. Noted British author, name used in an Edward Albee title   ————————————

13. American actor and comedian (*The Dick Van Dyke Show*)   ————————————

Moving Van

Each of the 30 definitions below refers to a word, name, or expression containing the letters VAN. For example: *To move forward* means to *adVANce*. How many of them can you come up with?

A score of 17 is good; 23 is excellent; 26 or more is enough to make you vain.

1. Disappear into thin air   _____

2. State in the eastern U.S.   _____

3. Destructive hoodlum; originally, a marauding ancient people of Europe   _____

4. Germane or pertinent; what some students think school isn't   _____

5. Jimmy Carter's Secretary of State   _____

6. Fearful and notorious Russian monarch   _____

7. Head start; superiority; term used in tennis   _____

8. TV comedian; star, with Mary Tyler Moore, of landmark 60's sitcom   _____

9. U.S. President, 1837–1841   _____

10. Major city in British Columbia, Canada   _____

11. Transient; ephemeral   _____

12. Element number 23   _____

13. Billy Graham, Billy Sunday, and Oral Roberts, e.g.   _____

14. Actress who played Lucille Ball's sidekick   _____

15. Organized train of cars, trucks, or pack animals

     _____

16. Ice cream flavor

     _____

17. Film starring Jack Lemmon and Juliet Mills; Italian word meaning *foreword*

     _____

18. Roman god of forests

     _____

19. Novel by William Makepeace Thackeray

     _____

20. Flemish painter, 1599–1641; beard bearing his name

     _____

21. Capital of Soviet Armenia

     _____

22. Invention or mechanical device; deceitful practice

     _____

23. Forefront; first line of an army; type of US missile

     _____

24. American millionaire; Nashville university bears his name

     _____

25. British actress (1888–1976) played in *Tom Jones* and *The Whisperers*

     _____

26. Conquer or defeat utterly

     _____

27. Huge American electronics manufacturer

     _____

28. Narrative poem by Henry Wadsworth Longfellow

     _____

29. European region straddling the Romanian-Hungarian border; famous as setting of *Dracula* and other horror stories

     _____

30. British actress, Oscar-winner for *Julia*

     _____

Watch It!

Each of the 34 clues below should suggest to you a term that contains the letters ATCH. For example, *A timepiece worn on the arm* would be a *wrist*WATCH. How many of them can you supply?

A score of 21 is good; 26 is an achievement; 31 means you're more than a MATCH for this quiz.

1. Quantity or accumulation of something   _____

2. Novel by J.D. Salinger with Holden Caufield as hero   _____

3. Lock on a door or gate   _____

4. Small suitcase; doctor's bag   _____

5. Alfred Hitchcock film starring Cary Grant   _____

6. Doorway on a ship; bring forth from egg   _____

7. Western U.S. railroad   _____

8. Code phrase; motto   _____

9. Axe, tomahawk   _____

10. Slang term meaning "certainly, of course"   _____

11. Legendary man-like beast in the Pacific Northwest   _____

12. Piece of cloth for mending   _____

13. Seize quickly; tear away from   _____

14. 1943 anti-Fascist film written by Lillian Hellman   _____

15. Teeth on a wheel or gear   _____

16. Roof of straw or reeds   _____

17. Position in baseball behind the batter   _____

18. Historic river port in Mississippi   _____

19. Superstition about bad luck to a smoker   _____

20. Photographer's advice to a poser   _____

21. Metal framework on front of a locomotive   _____

22. 1958 Perry Como hit   _____

23. Kind of beetle, thought to portend someone's demise   _____

24. To send out; promptness   _____

25. Idiom meaning haphazard; type of wrestling   _____

26. Mar; abrade; score   _____

27. Carl Perkins song on Beatles' *Something New* album   _____

28. Sample piece of cloth or fabric   _____

29. Province in Canada   _____

30. Joseph Heller's satiric novel of World War II   _____

31. Poor family in Dickens' *A Christmas Carol*   _____

32. Female antagonist of *One Flew Over the Cuckoo's Nest*   _____

33. Thornton Wilder play and film, basis for *Hello, Dolly!*   _____

34. 1965 film starring Sidney Poitier and Elizabeth Hartman   _____

It's about Time

Below, you will find 21 expressions, phrases, or names. Each one of these should suggest to you another expression which contains the word TIME. For example, a *Train Schedule* is a TIME*table*.

A score of 13 is good; 16 is first-rate; and 18 is top-notch.

1. Jazz _____
2. Very rapidly _____
3. A chronometer _____
4. A novel by Thomas Wolfe _____
5. Popular song classic _____
6. Aphorism about delay and the ocean _____
7. To deceive a spouse or lover _____
8. Repeatedly _____
9. Hit song in *Porgy and Bess* _____
10. Official world chronometry _____
11. Workers punch it _____
12. Without end _____
13. Broadway & 42nd Street _____
14. Play by William Saroyan _____
15. Fellow always ready for fun _____
16. Personification of chronometry _____
17. Immemorially _____
18. Double pay _____
19. Backward in adopting things _____
20. How to begin a fairy tale _____
21. To be in jail _____

Sally Forth

All 60 of the terms to be identified in this quiz contain the letters SAL. For example, "Pay for employment" would be sALary. Using the clues given, how many of them can you come up with?

A score of 25 is good; 35 is excellent; and 45 earns you a 21-gun sALute.

1. Fish with pink meat   _____

2. Pertaining to the nose   _____

3. The capital of Oregon; Massachusetts city famed for witch trials   _____

4. Most common spice   _____

5. Time of youthful inexperience   _____

6. Practice session   _____

7. Spittle   _____

8. Discoverer of anti-polio vaccine   _____

9. American actor who was murdered (*Rebel Without Cause, Exodus*)   _____

10. Germane; pertinent; outstanding   _____

11. Bar; gin mill   _____

12. Biblical poem   _____

13. Capital of Utah   _____

14. Novel by Gustave Flaubert set in ancient Carthage   _____

15. Newt   _____

16. Book of prayers   _____

17. Regarded with a measure of skepticism or suspicion   _____

18. Heroine of *Cabaret*   _____

19. American actress (*Auntie Mame, Mourning Becomes Electra*), 1911–1976 _____

20. Italian garlic sausage _____

21. The capital of Zimbabwe/Rhodesia _____

22. Barrage of rockets, shells, etc. _____

23. World-famous Spanish cellist (1876–1973) _____

24. Waldorf or Caesar, e.g. _____

25. Dark igneous rock, often forming natural columns _____

26. Formal opening _____

27. Type of food poisoning _____

28. Pulitzer-winning play by Arthur Miller _____

29. Region of ancient Greece _____

30. Feudal servant _____

31. Nation of Central America _____

32. Idiom for person(s) with sterling qualities _____

33. Rebellious son of King David _____

34. Arabian breed of dog _____

35. Capital of Tanzania _____

36. Biblical dancer who asked the head of John the Baptist _____

37. Famous fan-dancer _____

38. Anti-Caesar epic by Roman poet Lucan _____

39. Tray, especially of gold or silver _____

40. French explorer of North America   ——————————

41. Italian dish of veal and ham
    (the name means literally
    "jumps in the mouth")   ——————————

42. Dictator of Portugal from 1932 to 1968 ——————————

43. Ancient and medieval dulcimer-like
    musical instrument   ——————————

44. Reclamation of garbage, junk,
    wrecked ships, etc.   ——————————

45. French literary drawing room   ——————————

46. Adjective used to describe
    unbecoming complexion   ——————————

47. Swedish city   ——————————

48. A highly seasoned stew-like dish   ——————————

49. Healthful   ——————————

50. Moslem leader who fought Crusaders   ——————————

51. Pertaining to the back   ——————————

52. Surrealist artist   ——————————

53. Author of *The Catcher in the Rye*   ——————————

54. Sweet white Italian wine   ——————————

55. Birthplace of Mozart   ——————————

56. Religious, philanthropic organization

57. Author of *Bambi*   ——————————

58. Capital of Israel   ——————————

59. Pornographic; lustful   ——————————

60. Executed third wife of
    Roman emperor Claudius   ——————————

The Lowdown

All 40 of the following clues should suggest to you words, names, or expressions that contain the letters LOW. How many of them can you fill in?

A score of 20 is good; 27 is excellent; 34 should leave you with a warm gLOW!

1. Underneath   _____

2. Canary-colored   _____

3. Buffoon, circus comic   _____

4. Move smoothly like water _____

5. Permit; tolerate   _____

6. Cushion   _____

7. Member of a fraternal society, originated in 18th-century England _____

8. Blossom; bloom   _____

9. Frown; scowl   _____

10. Work action just short of a strike _____

11. Ingest orally; type of bird _____

12. American poet (1807–1882) _____

13. With little depth or personality _____

14. Idiom meaning person of least importance in a hierarchy _____

15. Red-baiting term of the McCarthy era _____

16. Tree with drooping, almost vine-like leaves _____

17. Collective term for Holland, Belgium, and Luxembourg _____

18. Fat by-product used in candle-making _____

20

19. What Isaiah would have us turn our
 swords into _____

20. Ship which landed at Plymouth Rock _____

21. Softened by experience; mature _____

22. Pursue; come after _____

23. Early Hollywood sex symbol _____

24. 60's term for hippies _____

25. Moving below normal speed _____

26. Confection toasted at campfires _____

27. Blacksmith's instrument for forcing air
 into forge _____

28. Clifford Odets' play about Noah and
 the ark _____

29. Empty, superficial _____

30. Nobel Prize-winning American
 novelist _____

31. Founder of the Girl Scouts _____

32. Bob Dylan song made popular by
 Peter, Paul, and Mary _____

33. 1959 film starring Doris Day _____

34. Structure for execution by hanging _____

35. English dramatist and poet,
 1564-1593 _____

36. Famous Negro spiritual _____

37. Person lacking cultivated intellectual
 tastes _____

38. American poet, *Patterns*, e.g. _____

39. Forgive because of mitigating
 circumstances _____

40. Novelist, author of *Under the Volcano* _____

Big Mac

All 40 items defined in this quiz have in common the letters MAC. For example: *Drugstore* would be *phar*MAC*y*. Using the clues below, how many of the words, names or expressions can you supply?

A score of 25 is good; 30 is excellent; 35 establishes your supreMACy in word games.

1. Digestive organ _____

2. Brightly colored parrot _____

3. Late American general ("I shall
   return") _____

4. Cord knotted in designs _____

5. Host of *The Original Amateur Hour* _____

6. Wide-bladed hacking knife sometimes
   used as weapon _____

7. Asphalt-like road surfacing material _____

8. Spotless; pristine; unblemished _____

9. Type of noodle _____

10. Kind of shrub, sometimes poisonous _____

11. H.G. Well's classic science fiction
    novel _____

12. Famous New York department store,
    the largest in the world _____

13. Kind of fish: "Holy _____!" _____

14. Facial distortion; look of pain or
    displeasure _____

15. Suggestive taste or flavor; slang for
    kiss or slap _____

16. Famous drama by Shakespeare _____

17. Doily for back or arms of chair
    to prevent soiling _____

18. Symphonic poem by Saint-Saëns _____

19. TV series with Rock Hudson and
    Susan St. James _____

20. British statesman and labor leader;
    former prime minister _____

21. Confederate ironclad, more correctly
    known as the *Virginia* _____

22. Starved; reduced to skin and bones _____

23. Diacritical mark signifying
    a long vowel _____

24. Notorious Italian political theorist
    (1469-1527) _____

25. Ancient land of Alexander the Great,
    now part of Yugoslavia _____

26. Kind of nut associated with Hawaii _____

27. Anti-hero of *The Threepenny Opera* _____

28. Portuguese colony in Asia,
    near Hong Kong _____

29. Slang for "dollar" _____

30. Jewish patriots of the
    2nd century B.C. _____

31. New York shop noted for
    fine housewares _____

32. Small pastry made of coconut
    and almonds _____

33. Sentimental Irish song _____

34. Son of Penelope and Odysseus   _____

35. A kind of raincoat, or apple   _____

36. Drama by Racine about Hector's wife   _____

37. American poet, author of Pulitzer
    Prize winning *Conquistador*   _____

38. Character who fulfilled the witches'
    prophecy that Macbeth would not
    be overcome by man born of
    woman, nor until Birnam forest
    came to Dunsinane   _____

39. Short story with long title
    by Ernest Hemingway   _____

40. The 63rd year of a person's life   _____

Bellringers

Each of the 45 words or expressions defined below contains the letters BELL. For example: *Colloquial term for stomach* would be BELLy. How many can you identify?

A score of 20 is good; 30 is excellent; 40 really rings the BELL.

1. Nursery rhyme   _____

2. Well-known soup manufacturer   _____

3. Waging war, or likely to do so   _____

4. Famous Philadelphia tourist attraction   _____

5. Jimmy Carter's Attorney General   _____

6. The hit of the party, the loveliest
   lady present   _____

7. Roar in anger or pain   _____

8. Author of Utopian novel
   Looking Backward   _____

9. Clown on TV's *The Howdy Doody
   Show*   _____

10. Hemingway novel made into
    1943 film starring Gary Cooper   _____

11. Another name for deadly nightshade   _____

12. Adjective for many beautiful Southern
    mansions (Latin for "pre-war")   _____

13. Risible dive in which stomach hits the
    water first   _____

14. Family of Venetian Renaissance
    painters   _____

15. Leader or leading indicator   _____

16. Robert Redford's character in
    The Way We Were
    _____

17. To decorate or exaggerate
    _____

18. Warlike; hostile; bullying
    _____

19. Nickname for the phone company
    _____

20. John Hersey novel made into
    1945 film
    _____

21. Entertainer in a Turkish nightclub.
    _____

22. Turn-of-the-century xenophobic
    movement in China
    _____

23. Flamboyant ex-Congresswoman from
    New York City
    _____

24. In Greek mythology, tamer of Pegasus
    and slayer of the Chimaera
    _____

25. Canadian-American novelist, winner
    of the 1976 Nobel Prize
    _____

26. Kind-hearted madam in
    Gone with the Wind
    (played by Ona Munson in film)
    _____

27. Weights used in body-building
    _____

28. Colloquial for the navel
    _____

29. Film starring Jimmy Stewart and Kim
    Novak (as a modern witch)
    _____

30. Mild expletive
    _____

31. 1794 Pennsylvania uprising against
    Federal excise taxes
    _____

32. 1960 film about Franklin Delano
    Roosevelt
    _____

33. Star of #32
    _____

34. 1945 film starring Bing Crosby and
    Ingrid Bergman   _____

35. American novelist, author of *Jurgen*   _____

36. Italian composer of *Norma* and
    I Puritani   _____

37. Novel by the late Sylvia Plath   _____

38. Trousers worn by sailors   _____

39. Eye make-up manufacturer   _____

40. Hotel employee who carries luggage   _____

41. German measles   _____

42. Woman writer who did exposé of
    the Standard Oil Company in
    McClure's Magazine, around 1900   _____

43. Song from *Guys and Dolls*   _____

44. Luis Buñuel film starring
    Catherine Deneuve (1967)   _____

45. Fine Irish pottery   _____

Him and Her

Each of the 35 terms defined below contains either the letters HER or the letters HIM. The blanks tell you the number of missing letters. For example: *Female parent* would be *mot*HER.

 A score of 18 is good; 24 is excellent; 30 makes you the Person of the Year!

1. __ HIM __ __ __   Santa Claus' means of entry

2. __ HER __ __ __   Curative treatment

3. __ HIM   Arbitrary notion; yen

4. __ HER __ __ __   County law-enforcement officer

5. __ __ __ HIM __   Japanese delicacy of raw fish

6. __ __ HER   Anesthetic first used by
                           Crawford W. Long

7. __ HIM __ __ __ __ __   Small variety of ape

8. __ HER __ __ __   Container for keeping liquids
                           hot or cold

9. __ HIM __   Bell; ring out

10. __ HER __ __ __ __
    __ __ __ __ __ __   Robin Hood's sylvan retreat

11. "__ __ __ __ __ __ __ __HIM"   Male chauvinist song from
                            My Fair Lady

12. __ HER __ __ __   Cucumber variety often used
                            for pickles

13. __ HIM __ __ __   Finger-shielding device used in sewing

14. __ __ __ __ __ __ __ __ __
    __ __ __ __ __
    __ __ __ HER __ __   Morris West novel
                            about a Russian pope

15. HIM _ _ _ _ _ _   Vast mountain range in Asia

16. _ HER _ _ _ _   Love; appreciate; be grateful for

17. _ HIM _ _ _ _ _ _   Mythical; visionary; imaginary

18. _ HER _ _ _ _ _   French seaport on the English Channel

19. _ _ _ _ HIM _ _ _ _   Greek physicist and inventor (275-212 B.C.)

20. _ _ _ _ _ HER   Climatic conditions

21. _ HIM _ _ _ _   Whine; mournful cry

22. _ _ HER _ _ _ _   Innate, characteristic

23. _ _ _ _ _ HIM _   City devastated by atomic attack August 6, 1945

24. _ _ _ _ _ _ _ _ _ HER   Patron saint for travelers

25. _ HIM _ _ _ _   Gleam faintly

26. _ HER _ _ _ _   Union general who burned Atlanta during his march to the sea

27. _ _ _ HIM _   Japanese writer Yukio _____, a famous suicide and author of *The Sailor Who Fell from Grace with the Sea*

28. _ _ _ _ HER   Jungle cat

29. HER _ _ _ _ _ _   Greek hero noted for his strength

30. _ HER _ _   Type of angel; adorable child

31. _ HIM _ _   Quaintness; fanciful notion

32. _ _ _ HER   Dry up

33. HIM _ _ _ _ _   Head of the Gestapo in Nazi Germany

34. _ HER _ _ _ _ _   English designer of fine furniture, 1751-1806

35. _ HIM _ _   A jazz dance

In Apple-Pie Order

Ever since Eve ate the "forbidden fruit" and was expelled from Eden, the apple has fascinated mankind. Below are a dozen questions about apples of renown. How many can you identify correctly?

A score of six is peachy; nine or more shows great *apple*titude.

1. Proverbially, one a day keeps this person away

2. This legendary hero shot an apple off his son's head

3. This American pioneer earned his nickname because he planted apple seeds widely

4. This term originated in Greek mythology where the golden apple was "for the most beautiful"

5. This fairy tale character was drugged with an apple by the wicked witch

6. The gift of an apple symbolizes appreciation for this person's work

7. This person's kindnesses are not too altruistic

8. A part of the larynx

9. Where does the expression "apple of my eye" come from?

10. What expression would you use to tell someone not to disrupt things?

11. A brandy made from apples

12. This English physicist and Nobel Prize winner inspired the development of radar

Calculated Risk

Each of the 50 clues below define a term that contains the letters CAL. How many of them can you come up with?

    A score of 25 is good; 32 is excellent; 38 or better is doing fantastiCALly well!

1. Units of heat; something dieters count   _____

2. Nearby; close to home; slow train   _____

3. Most populous of the 50 states   _____

4. Of government; the kind of animal man is   _____

5. Kind of organ; the Muse of epic poetry   _____

6. Campus in Pasadena   _____

7. Placid, serene   _____

8. A Broadway show with song and dance   _____

9. Widow of Humphrey Bogart, star of *Murder on the Orient Express*   _____

10. Picture or design transfered from paper   _____

11. Mad Roman emperor (37-41 A.D.)   _____

12. Type of onion   _____

13. Young cow; part of the leg   _____

14. Site of the crucifixion   _____

15. Moving staircase   _____

16. Element number 20, found in bones and teeth _____

17. 30th United States President _____

18. Cord connecting fetus to mother _____

19. Important; vital; censorious _____

20. Cotton fabric often used in bed linens _____

21. A chart or register that shows dates _____

22. Catastrophic; disastrous _____

23. Unruly; defiant _____

24. Burn, especially with steam _____

25. Old name for Scotland _____

26. Sensible; reasonable; predictable _____

27. Name for collaborationist Southerners during Reconstruction _____

28. Alfalfa, Spanky *et al.* _____

29. Site of the University of Alabama _____

30. Heckler's noise _____

31. Long, long word popularized by Mary Poppins _____

32. Hair-covered part of the head _____

33. Slander; disgrace; invective _____

34. Existing only in legend or fiction _____

35. Surgeon's knife _____

36. Exercises; work-outs _____

37. Hallucinogenic drug made from peyote _____

38. Type of higher mathematics _____

39. Father of Presbyterianism   _____

40. Type of shellfish; term used in cooking   _____

41. Beautiful handwriting   _____

42. Relating to sight, often used with
    "illusion"   _____

43. Bachelor's degree   _____

44. Cold; unfeeling; unsympathetic   _____

45. Opposite; in total contrast   _____

46. Character in Shakespeare's
    The Tempest   _____

47. Late Beatles album featuring "All You
    Need Is Love"   _____

48. Remove someone from office;
    remember   _____

49. Up-to-date, pertinent, germane   _____

50. Poison ivy remedy   _____

How in the World?

Each of the 40 definitions below should suggest to you a name, word or expression that contains the letters HOW. For example: *To display or demonstrate* is SHOW. HOW many of them can you come up with?

A score of 20 is good; 27 is excellent; 34 is real SHOWmanship!

1. Scream; cry; poem by
   Allen Ginsburg   _____

2. Bathe under falling water;
   engagement party   _____

3. Lyricist for "The Battle Hymn of
   the Republic"   _____

4. Slang for food   _____

5. 1971 film directed by Peter
   Bogdanovich   _____

6. Official nickname for Missouri   _____

7. Buffoonish sportscaster   _____

8. Well-known question posed by
   Elizabeth Barrett Browning   _____

9. Actor who plays Richie
   Cunningham on *Happy Days*   _____

10. Elocutionist's vowel exercise   _____

11. They bring May flowers   _____

12. Inventor of the sewing machine   _____

13. Type of soup made with fish   _____

14. Eliza's tirade song from
    My Fair Lady   _____

15. 1964 Stanley Kubrick film satirizing
    the nuclear age
    (full title)   _____

16. 34th U.S. President   _____

17. 1977 film starring Lily Tomlin
    and Art Carney   _____

18. One way of voting   _____

19. Classic TV comedy series starring
    Sid Caesar and Imogene Coca   _____

20. Saddle for an elephant   _____

21. 1963 film about the pioneer
    movement   _____

22. 27th U.S. President, later
    Chief Justice   _____

23. Bespectacled character in *Pogo*
    comic strip   _____

24. 1967 Broadway musical about the
    stock market   _____

25. Cecil B. De Mille circus film,
    Best Picture of 1952   _____

26. Heavy artillery piece   _____

27. Puppet in cowboy garb,
    companion of Buffalo Bob Smith   _____

28. British actor, he played Ashley in
    Gone with the Wind   _____

29. Song from *Annie, Get Your Gun*,
    the unofficial anthem of the
    entertainment industry   _____

30. Film directed by John Ford, based
    on work by Richard Llewellyn   _____

31. The final test   _____

32. American playwright, *They Knew What They Wanted*, e.g.   _____

33. Preschool language activity   _____

34. American writer and critic, associated with *Atlantic Monthly* and *Harper's Magazine*   _____

35. By a method not known or understood   _____

36. Dale Carnegie's classic primer for success   _____

37. An excellent work, worthy of being displayed   _____

38. Musical based on work by Edna Ferber   _____

39. Popular Chinese-American dish   _____

40. Novel by E.M. Forster about the Schlegels and the Wilcoxes   _____

Daydreaming

Below are 50 definitions, each of which should suggest to you a name, phrase or title containing the word DAY. It should take you something less than forever and a day to get them.

A score of 25 is good; 35 is excellent; 42 makes it a red-letter DAY!

1. Autobiographical drama by
   Eugene O'Neill _____

2. Famous last line of
   Gone with the Wind _____

3. Proverb meaning, "Things take time." _____

4. First day of Lent _____

5. Top-rated TV show featuring
   the Fonz _____

6. "What is so rare as . . ." _____

7. Irish tenor, Jack Benny's sidekick _____

8. Character in *Robinson Crusoe* _____

9. 1969 film, with Genevieve Bujold
   as the wife of Henry VIII _____

10. June 6, 1944 _____

11. 1962 film starring Jack Lemmon and
    Lee Remick _____

12. Joan Baez' autobiography; dawn _____

13. Landmark Beatles song, finale of
    "Sgt. Pepper" album _____

14. Novel by Nathanael West, and film
    starring Donald Sutherland,
    about Hollywood in the 30s _____

15. Miserable period of July and August   _____

16. Novel and film about an assassination
    plot against DeGaulle   _____

17. Term for the 1916 uprising in Ireland   _____

18. Christian term for the end of time   _____

19. The day when one receives wages   _____

20. Short novel by Solzhenitsyn   _____

21. Classic science-fiction film starring
    Michael Rennie   _____

22. February 22, 1732   _____

23. Novel by Knebel and Bailey, made
    into film starring Burt Lancaster
    and Frederic March, about an
    attempted military coup in the U.S.   _____

24. City in Ohio   _____

25. Israeli military leader   _____

26. Early hit by The Mamas and the Papas   _____

27. 1976 film starring Al Pacino
    as a bank robber   _____

28. July 4th in the USA   _____

29. Blond movie star, the "eternal virgin"   _____

30. July 14th in France   _____

31. "Shall I compare thee..."   _____

32. Famous give-away show of the 1950s   _____

33. 1971 film starring Peter Finch and
    Glenda Jackson   _____

34. Centuries-old child's rhyme,
    mnemonic device for reckoning
    length of months   _____

35. Broadway hit about reincarnation, made into film with Barbara Streisand and Yves Montand _____

36. Play and film by Kurt Vonnegut, Jr. _____

37. 1960 film starring Melina Mercouri as a Greek prostitute _____

38. Disturbances in Chicago in October, 1969, led by the Weathermen; translation of Catholic hymn *Dies Irae* _____

39. Solo by Paul McCartney on Beatles' *Rubber Soul* album _____

40. Jules Verne novel; Oscar-winning Best Picture of 1956 _____

41. She has far to go _____

42. TGIF _____

43. Famous publisher and bookseller _____

44. Author of *Life with Father* _____

45. Length of time of the Owl and the Pussycat's sea journey _____

46. English scientist who formulated laws of electrolysis _____

47. Proverb meaning, "Even the downtrodden have times of joy or revenge." _____

48. Newspaper column by Eleanor Roosevelt _____

49. Jewish holiday of Yom Kippur _____

50. Expression meaning to stop working _____

Boning Up

All 50 definitions below identify words, names or phrases that contain the letters BON. For example: *Household cleaner* would be BON *Ami*. How many of them can you fill in?

A score of 25 is good; 35 is excellent; 45 proves you're no BONehead.

1. Link, connector; type of negotiable instruments

    _____

2. Charcoal; element number 6

    _____

3. Extra dividend

    _____

4. Slavery

    _____

5. Ex-husband of Cher

    _____

6. Strip of cloth used for tying things attractively

    _____

7. Type of lady's hat; in England, a car's hood

    _____

8. Suave; dashing; cultured

    _____

9. Capital of West Germany

    _____

10. Agent 007 created by Ian Fleming

    _____

11. Japanese dwarf tree

    _____

12. Sliding member of a band's brass section

    _____

13. Kentucky corn whiskey

    _____

14. Symbol of piracy, or of poison

    _____

15. Annual football game in Houston

    _____

16. Goof; error

    _____

17. Type of ape

    _____

18. Long-running TV Western starring Lorne Greene _____

19. Wanderer; rover; itinerant _____

20. Admit freely _____

21. Jet-black wood _____

22. Disease which ravaged Europe in 14th century _____

23. Conflagration for celebration _____

24. Western film starring John Wayne and Joanne Dru _____

25. Type of African antelope, or drum _____

26. Early 19th-century ruler of France and conqueror of Europe _____

27. Legitimate; on the level; for real _____

28. Candy with cream filling _____

29. A song of the Confederacy _____

30. Legal phrase meaning "for the common good" _____

31. Author of *The Decline and Fall of the Roman Empire* _____

32. Ship commanded by John Paul Jones _____

33. West African nation, capital Libreville _____

34. Much-parodied song about a faraway lover _____

35. Tuna-like fish _____

36. A witticism (Fr.) _____

37. An innkeeper _____

38. University of Paris _____

39. Slang term for a surgeon   _____

40. Subject of disagreement   _____

41. French painter, noted for her
    pictures of animals, 1822-1899   _____

42. Farewell wish for someone taking a
    trip   _____

43. An aperitif wine   _____

44. Porterhouse or club steak   _____

45. Family name of Giotto, famous
    Florentine painter and architect   _____

46. Hit tune of 1929   _____

47. Warren Beatty and Faye Dunaway
    in movie about two underworld
    characters   _____

48. Term for applying political pressure   _____

49. British slang for crazy   _____

50. Used in dating archaelogical finds   _____

In Cold Blood

Two sisters were married. The two couples jointly occupied a single apartment. The men, apart from being brothers-in-law, were otherwise unrelated.

One night, while both men were asleep, one of the girls said to her sister: "Come with me." She led her into the chamber where the two men were sleeping, and having approached her own husband, she drew a dagger and plunged it into his vitals. He awoke, shouting in his death agony: "You are murdering me!"

His brother-in-law, awakened by his cries, heard the woman announce coldly, "Yes, that's what I intend to do," and saw her again plunge the poniard up to its hilt into the victim's heart.

All the foregoing facts were established at the trial, not only by the evidence of the accused's sister and brother-in-law, but by the confession of the defendant herself. The jury duly brought in a verdict of "Guilty of murder in the first degree."

The judge stated that the verdict was unimpeachable. While deploring the depravity of the defendant, he nevertheless stated to a crowded courtroom that under the law he found it impossible to pronounce sentence upon her. The accused then walked off scot-free.

Now take it for granted that the trial was held in due conformity with legal requirements. Take it for granted that the verdict could not be set aside for any legal technicality, and furthermore, take it for granted that the judge was fully competent and exercised unimpeachable judgment. In short, the difficulty did not arise from any deficiencies in either the processes of the law or the presiding tribunal. The dilemma arose solely out of the circumstances of the case.

WHAT LOGICAL REASON COULD THE
JUDGE HAVE FOR REFUSING TO PRONOUNCE
SENTENCE UPON THE MURDERER?

The Municipal Railways

The illustration shows the plan of a city surrounded by pentagonal fortifications. Five railroad companies are clamoring for a concession to run a railway into the city. After deliberating, the mayor announces, "Let every one of them have a concession—but the line of one company must never cross the line of another!"

The letters in the diagram represent the five railroad companies, and indicate just where each line must enter the city, and where the terminal belonging to that line must be located.

Trace out the route for the line A to A, B to B, C to C, and so on, so that one line does not cross another, or pass through another company's terminal.

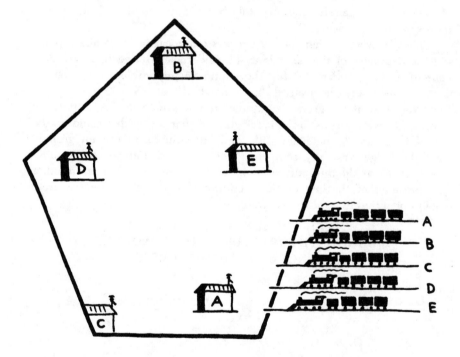

The Dead Tourist

Mr. and Mrs. Samuel Elkins, wealthy society folks, went on a trip to Switzerland to enjoy some mountain climbing.

A few weeks later, the attractive Mrs. Elkins, shrouded in heavy black, returned to her home in Boston, a widow. Mr. Elkins had missed his step while on a climbing expedition, and had been precipitated headlong down a steep ravine to a horrible death at the base of the mountain. It was a terrible accident and a terrible ordeal for the stricken Mrs. Elkins, who was with him at the time and witnessed the tragedy.

About a month after her return, her friends, who had given her their deepest sympathy, were astounded to hear that she had been indicted for the murder of her husband. But they were more shocked when Mrs. Elkins broke down and confessed!

The police had received the tip-off from a certain Mr. Harper, head of a well-known travel agency. Mr. Harper had never left the United States.

HOW DID HE DEDUCE THAT MRS. ELKINS
HAD MURDERED HER HUSBAND?

The Lost Coin

WHO IS ENTITLED TO THE COIN?

The Island of Ko

On the island of Ko there are three types of inhabitants, physically indistinguishable from one another. They are known as the Reds, the Greens, and the Half-Breeds.

A Red, when asked a question, invariably gives a truthful answer; a Green invariably gives an untruthful answer; a Half-Breed alternately lies and tells the truth, though one cannot tell whether his first answer will be a truthful one or not.

Three inhabitants—a Red, a Green, and a Half-Breed—were lounging on the beach. Their names (not necessarily respectively) were Tom, Dick, and Harry. A traveler accosted the first one and the following dialogue ensued:

"What is your name?"

"Tom, sir."

"Are you a Red, a Green, or a Half-Breed?"

"Green, sir."

"What is the name of your Red friend?"

"Dick, sir."

WHAT ARE THE NAMES OF THE RED,
THE GREEN, AND THE HALF-BREED?

The Steel Beam

A steel beam balances on a scale with three-quarters of a beam and a three-quarter-pound weight.

HOW MUCH DOES THE BEAM WEIGH?

Three Sons

Smith, Sr., Brown, Sr., and Jones, Sr., each had a grown son. We may call the sons Smith, Jr., Brown, Jr., and Jones, Jr. One of the Juniors was a politician; another, a banker; and the third, a lawyer.

    (1) The lawyer frequently played tennis with his father.

    (2) Brown, Jr., called the politician a socialist.

    (3) The politician's father played golf every Wednesday with another of the older men.

    (4) Smith, Sr., had been a paralytic from youth.

WHAT WAS THE NAME OF THE LAWYER?

The Vanished Coin

The eight members of an exclusive society in London known as the Collector's Club are each considered experts and connoisseurs of *objets d'art*, stamps, and coins.

The Club does not admit outsiders to its meetings, and even bars waiters from serving the bowls of fruit which invariably grace the long table at which the informal, fortnightly discussions are held.

One day, one of the members met an acquaintance who also was a collector of coins. The friend, who had heard much about the famed discussions at the Club, was so insistent about being taken to a meeting that the member, succumbing to his friend's entreaties, obtained permission to have him attend.

During the meeting, Mr. Grant Lewis, a coin collector just returned from a Continental tour, exhibited his prize find—an ancient, rare Phoenician coin. The coin passed from hand to hand and was closely scrutinized by all those present, amidst a continual barrage of questions directed at the proud Lewis. Lewis, urged to expatiate on the history of his rarity, surrendered to the importunities of his fellow members. He requested the silver piece be handed back to him in order to point out certain peculiarities; but no one had the coin.

Each averred he had passed it to another, so that from the maze of statements it was impossible to determine who actually had the coin last. Every inch of the carpet was examined, but the coin seemed to have vanished into thin air. Everyone volubly urged calm, thus indicating how upset the members actually were. Fear lest the scandal besmirch the honor of the venerable Collector's Club crowded out the suspicion that perhaps a fraud was being perpetrated, for the coin was worth a fabulous sum.

Finally, the demand was made that everyone submit to a personal examination. The suggestion was taken up and seconded with willingness by all—that is, all except the stranger. He demurred resolutely. Not only would he not submit to a search of his person, but he steadfastly refused to divulge any reason for his apparently stubborn refusal. The chairman threatened to inform the police. As the words fell from his lips, Grant Lewis reached forth nervously into the silver bowl for an apple. As he drew the fruit away, there to his amazement, at the bottom of the bowl,

he saw his prize coin. Confusion succeeded bewilderment; and profuse apologies poured forth upon the stranger, who rose to explain.

The explanation for his refusing to be searched and refusing further to give a reason for his attitude was sound.

WHAT SENSIBLE AND LOGICAL EXPLANATION DID THE STRANGER OFFER?

Narrow Escape

Mr. Drake was driving his car along a straight highway in Florida which led due north to his destination, a town 20 miles north of his starting point. When he had gone approximately 19 miles, a fast-moving car passed his. As a result, his car was forced a couple of yards off the highway, thereby scraping its side against some protruding bushes.

Drake stopped his car, and as he was looking out the window to ascertain whether any noticeable damage had been done by the bushes, he judged from the position of the sun that it was late in the afternoon and that he would have to hurry. A couple of minutes later, he arrived at his destination, happy in the thought that he had escaped a possibly serious accident.

WHAT IS THE FALLACY IN THE ABOVE STORY?

It Really Happened One Night

A charming hedonist, whom we'll call Winston, came home one night at about 2 A.M., rather tired after the revels of the night. He went to bed directly. About twenty minutes later, he got up, opened the local telephone book, and looked up the number of one Gerald Malcolm. He called, and a sweet soprano answered.

"Hello! Is this Mrs. Malcolm?" queried Winston.

"Yes."

"He's asleep."

"But it's very important!" Winston insisted.

"Important! Well, hold the wire a moment and I'll awaken him."

"Young Winston glued his ear to the receiver long enough to hear Mrs. Malcolm walking off spouseward. *Then he deliberately hung up!*

Now ruling out any hoax or wager, and hypothecating that Winston had never previously met or communicated with either Mr. or Mrs. Malcolm, and assuming that Winston acted premeditatedly and planned *everything* he did:

WHAT MOTIVE CAN YOU ASSIGN FOR HIS ACTION?

The Dormitory Puzzle

There are six rooms on the floor of a girl's dormitory. Each room is occupied by a girl from a different city. It is up to you to figure out, from the clues below, the names of the six girls, which room each occupies, and what city each one comes from.

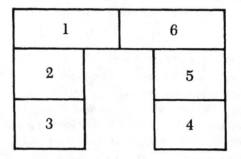

1. Kim is from New York

2. The girl from Chicago occupies Room 4

3. Lisa does not have a corner room

4. A Kansas City girl lives between Kim and Tina

5. The girl in Room 3 comes from Los Angeles

6. Ruth occupies Room 6

7. Mona occupies Room 5

8. A Cleveland girl is in the room between girls from Chicago and Cincinnati

9. Tina lives across the hall from Rita

The Football Tournament

An elimination tournament in football was held in which four colleges—
Trinity, Tufts, Temple, and Tulane—participated. The winners of the
first two games met in the third and final game to decide the championship. The colors of the various teams were brown, blue, red, and purple,
and the competing captains were Albie, Barry, Bill, and Ben, though not
necessarily respectively. The following facts are known:

(1) In the final game Albie's team made its only score by a touchdown on
the first play, but missed the point after touchdown.
(2) The red team lost to Tufts in the first game.
(3) Ben's team defeated Tulane 12 to 0.
(4) The captain of the purple team saved his team from being scoreless in
the third game by a 40-yard field goal.
(5) Ben's team did not play Trinity.
(6) Barry's team lost to the undefeated team.
(7) Albie did not see his former friend, the captain of the brown team.

**WHO DEFEATED WHOM IN THE PLAY-OFF, AND
BY WHAT SCORE? WHO WAS THE CAPTAIN OF EACH
TEAM? WHAT WAS THE COLOR OF EACH TEAM?**

Gamesmanship

Four women—Carol, Eloise, Gwen, and Joan—work for the same company. As it happens, each of these women is an expert in one of these games—backgammon, bridge, checkers, and tennis. But only some of the women know each other. Furthermore, even those who know each other do not necessarily play together.

You have only four clues to go by, but even with these skimpy facts, you should be able to figure out in which game each woman excels.

Using the chart below should help you reach the solution.

If you can solve this problem in 20 minutes, you must be an expert in games of logic; if you take less than that amount of time, you must be the one who makes up the logic games.

1. Gwen once played in a bridge tournament with the woman who is the expert in bridge.

2. Carol once persuaded the woman who excels in tennis to play tennis with her.

3. The backgammon champ and Carol are friends, but they have never played any sort of game together.

4. Neither Eloise nor the backgammon champ ever met Joan.

	Bridge	Tennis	Backgammon	Checkers
CAROL				
ELOISE				
GWEN				
JOAN				

54

The Forty-Two Beers

In Guatelavia, the standard dollar is worth 100¢. In the bordering country of Tinto, the standard dollar is also worth 100¢. In fact, both dollars contain the same gold equivalent and are of exact value.

However, because of conditions of foreign exchange, the Guatelavian dollar is worth only 90¢ in Tinto, while the Tintoese dollar is worth but 90¢ in Guatelavia.

One day a smart Yankee with an enormous thirst drops into a Guatelavian café and orders a 10¢ beer. He hands over the single Guatelavian dollar that he has in his pocket, and ask for 90¢ in change in Tintoese money. Since the Tintoese dollar is only worth 90¢ in Guatelavia, the barkeep gives him a full Tintoese dollar.

Whereupon our friend hops across the border and makes for the nearest saloon. He orders a beer and hands the bartender in Tinto a Tintoese dollar—the one he got in Guatelavia—demanding 90¢ change in Guatelavian money. Since, as aforesaid, the Guatelavian dollar is worth only 90¢ in Tinto, he receives a full Guatelavian dollar for his change.

Things look pretty bright for the Yankee, and he keeps up the transaction the whole day long, imbibing exactly 42 beers. When he is done, he finds that he has the same Guatelavian dollar he started out with.

Now apparently the Guatelavian café sold 21 beers at the ordinary price and made a profit; and apparently the Tintoese saloon sold 21 beers with a profit, and evidently the American financial wizard got 42 beers without expending a single penny . . . So the question remains:

WHO PAID FOR THEM THERE BEERS?

Count the Trains

CAN YOU ANSWER TOM'S QUESTION?

The Horse Trader

A horse trader brings a string of horses to a horse fair. As admission charge, he gives up one of his horses. At the fair, he sells one half of those remaining; and on the way out, he is charged one horse as a trading fee.

He proceeds to a second fair where like conditions prevail. There he pays one horse to get in, sells half of the horses he still has on hand, and pays a single horse as trading fee.

He proceeds to a third fair where like conditions prevail. Here, too, he pays one horse to get in, sells half of the horses he still has on hand, and pays a single horse as trading fee.

He then has one horse left on which to ride home with his proceeds.

HOW MANY HORSES DID HE START OUT WITH?

Boots

Mr. Cobblewell, a bootmaker, sold a pair of boots to a well-dressed stranger, who tendered a $50 bill in payment. As he had no change, Mr. Cobblewell went next door and had his friend Plaster, the druggist, change the bill. The price of the boots was $46. The stranger took his change and left.

Shortly afterwards Plaster appeared in Cobblewell's shop in a state of much agitation to explain that the $50 bill he had been given was counterfeit. Naturally, Cobblewell had no option but to replace it with a good $50 bill.

HOW MUCH HAS COBBLEWELL LOST?

The Lily Pond

A certain pond in Central America is a perfect circle twenty feet in diameter. Every year a magnificent water-lily appears in the exact center of the pond. The lily grows with a remarkable rapidity, doubling its area every day; at the end of exactly twenty-one days, the lily fills the entire area of the pond. Then it dies away and for twelve months no more is seen of it.

**AT THE END OF HOW MANY DAYS FROM ITS
FIRST APPEARANCE DOES THE LILY OCCUPY HALF
THE AREA OF THE POND?**

American Heritage

You may have thrilled to a game of *Cowboys and Indians* as a child, but how much do you know about the first Americans? Below are 13 questions about the American Indian. You have four choices; see how many you can get right.

A score of six makes you a brave warrior; eight makes you a good student of American history; and 10 must mean you're an Indian chief.

1. The indians left an opening in the top of their tepees to:
   - Let sun in
   - See the sky
   - Let smoke out
   - Air out the tepee

2. The Indians were so named because:
   - They resembled India ink
   - They were thought to have discovered the Indian Ocean
   - They were associated with Indian meal moths
   - They were thought to be East Indians

3. Wampum beads were used for money. But what special purpose did wampum belts serve?
   - They were the mark of the chief
   - They were exchanged when a peace treaty was signed
   - They were given to a boy during the puberty ceremony
   - They were worn by women for special religious ceremonies

4. How many war eagle tail feathers does the peace pipe of the Black-foot Indian have?
   - Four
   - Ten
   - Twelve
   - Sixteen

5. Which of the following did the Indians *not* make?
   - Ice cream
   - Chocolate
   - Hammock
   - Maple sugar

6. Which Indian tribe lived in the southwest?
   Navaho   Blackfoot
   Ottawa   Shasta

7. Lt. Colonel George A. Custer's last stand took place in 1876 at Little Bighorn River. He and his regiment were massacred in their attack on the:
   Sioux   Pueblo
   Comanche   Navaho

8. In 1887 Congress passed a law that provided each Indian with his own piece of land. This was the:
   Removal Act   Walker Act
   Dawes Act   Independent Act

9. For whom did the famous woman Indian, Sacajawea, act as guide?
   Samuel Hearne   Lewis and Clark
   Sir Alexander Mackenzie   Jedediah Strong Smith

10. The tub-shaped boat, made of willow covered with buffalo, used by tribes along the Missouri River is called a:
    Rowboat   Canoe
    Bullboat   Raft

11. About how many U.S. citizens today regard themselves as Indians?
    5 million   500,000
    2½ million   250,000

12. Which of the following American heroes is not an Indian?
    Ira Hayes   Oral Roberts
    Jim Thorpe   John Smith

13. We all are familiar with the slogan, "Remember the Alamo!" but what is it that is supposed to be remembered?
    The unsuccessful resistance of the Texans against Mexican
       leader Santa Anna
    The defeat of George Custer at Little Bighorn
    The last battle of the Indian Wars at Wounded Knee
       in 1890
    The slaughter of a group of pioneers in New Mexico
       by a Navaho tribe

Which Quipster?

The 20 *bons mots* below are by five famous authors—Robert Benchley, Ambrose Bierce, George Bernard Shaw, Mark Twain, and Oscar Wilde. When you stop laughing, see if you can identify who wrote what.

A score of 10 is good for laughs; 13 shows an active funny bone; and 17 must mean you're a stand-up comic.

1. Wagner's music is better than it sounds. _____

2. The fickleness of women I love is only equaled by the infernal constancy of the women who love me. _____

3. When I was young I used to think that money was the most important thing in life; now that I am old, I know it is. _____

4. I do most of my work sitting down; that's where I shine. _____

5. A classic is something that everybody wants to have read and nobody wants to read. _____

6. Bore: A person who talks when you wish him to listen. _____

7. Contentment is the smother of intention. _____

8. Drawing on my fine command of language, I said nothing. _____

9. Hatred is the coward's revenge for being intimidated. _____

10. George Moore wrote brilliant English until he discovered grammar.

    _____

11. It took me 15 years to discover I had no talent for writing, but I couldn't give it up because by that time I was too famous.

    _____

12. Democracy substitutes election by the incompetent many for appointment by the corrupt few.

    _____

13. I like criticism, but it must be my way.

    _____

14. A dog teaches a boy fidelity, perseverance, and to turn around three times before lying down.

    _____

15. To be good is noble, but to teach others how to be good is nobler— and less trouble.

    _____

16. To be positive: to be mistaken at the top of one's voice.

    _____

17. Let us not be too particular; it is better to have old secondhand diamonds than none at all.

    _____

18. There are two tragedies in life. One is not to get your heart's desire. The other is to get it.

    _____

19. To love oneself is the beginning of a lifelong romance.

    _____

20. Don't steal; thou'lt never thus compete
Successfully in business. Cheat.

    _____

Name That City

Sometimes, going to the movies is like taking an exotic trip. Can you complete the titles below by identifying the city that provides the setting for the movie? Choose your answers from the list of cities below. You may use the same city more than once.

A score of 16 makes you a movie buff; 20 shows you're well traveled; and 25 means you're a geographer.

1. *April in* _____
2. *Mission to* _____
3. *In Old* _____
4. *Death in* _____
5. *A Tree Grows in* _____
6. *Twenty Seconds Over* _____
7. *Last Train From* _____
8. *Boys From* _____
9. *The Last Tango in* _____
10. *Meet Me in* _____
11. *The* _____ *Story*
12. *Is* _____ *Burning?*
13. *Going* _____
14. *The Merchant of* _____
15. *When in* _____
16. *The Toast of* _____
17. *The Earl of* _____
18. *Mr. Smith Goes to* _____
19. *The Countess from* _____

20. *Two Gentlemen of* _____

21. *The* _____ *Kid*

22. *The Road to* _____

23. *Viva* _____

24. *Passenger to* _____

25. *Tales of* _____

26. *Judgment at* _____

27. *Fifty-five Days at* _____

28. _____ *Express*

29. _____ *Correspondent*

30. _____ *Calling*

BERLIN	**PARIS**
BROOKLYN	**PEKING**
CHICAGO	**PHILADELPHIA**
CINCINNATI	**ROME**
FRANKFORT	**SHANGHAI**
HOLLYWOOD	**MOROCCO**
HONG KONG	**SYRACUSE**
LAS VEGAS	**ST. LOUIS**
MADRID	**TOKYO**
MANHATTAN	**VENICE**
MOSCOW	**VERONA**
NEW YORK	**WASHINGTON**
NUREMBERG	

For The Love Of Music

If all the real and fictional characters in this quiz were gathered together you might have cacophony instead of harmony, but what an interesting collection of music-makers it would be! Your task to identify the musical instrument played by each character or on each occasion.

A score of 10 is pleasing; 14 is lyrical; and 17 is resounding.

What musical instrument was played:

1. By Orpheus, while wild animals listened?   _____

2. By the cat, while the cow jumped over the moon?   _____

3. By the Barber of Seville, in Rossini's opera?   _____

4. By the musician who was looking for *The Lost Chord*?   _____

5. By Sherlock Holmes, in his moments of relaxation?   _____

6. By Supiyawlet, in Kipling's *Road to Mandalay*?   _____

7. At the burial of Poor Cock Robin?   _____

8. By David, who slew the giant Goliath?   _____

9. By Nanki-Poo, the wandering minstrel in *The Mikado*?   _____

10. During the mariner's tale, in *Rime of the Ancient Mariner*?   _____

11. By Nero, while Rome burned?   _____

66

12. By Frederick the Great, who was a virtuoso and composer? _____

13. By Mother Hubbard's dog, in the famous nursery rhyme? _____

14. By the three soldiers in the famous painting *Spirit of '76?* _____

15. By the Owl who eloped with the Pussy Cat? _____

16. By President Harry Truman? _____

17. By the high priests to crumble the walls of Jericho? _____

18. By angels, in Renaissance paintings? _____

19. By Benny Goodman, jazz musician who also performed in classical music concerts? _____

20. Throughout the score of the movie *The Third Man?* _____

Color Me!

The 35 movie titles listed below have something in common. Each title has a color word which has been omitted in this quiz. Can you restore the color to these titles? Give yourself one point for each correct answer.

A score of 25 is worthy of a movie buff; 30 or more shows a great palette for movies.

1. _____ Submarine

2. _____ Mansions

3. _____ Narcissus

4. _____ finger

5. _____ Pimpernel

6. _____ Cliffs of Dover

7. _____ Beauty

8. _____ Heat

9. The _____ Shoes

10. The _____ Angel

11. The _____ Harvest

12. The _____ Cross

13. The _____ Hill Mob

14. The _____ Gardenia

15. The _____ Swan

16. The _____ Tattoo

17. The _____ Rush

18. The _____ Badge of Courage

19. The Girl in the _____ Velvet Swing

20. The Solid _____ Cadillac

21. The Picture of Dorian _____

22. The Man in the _____ Flannel Suit

23. The Corn Is _____

24. The Moon Is _____

25. The Woman in _____

26. A Patch of _____

27. Bad Day at _____ Rock

28. She Wore a _____ Ribbon

29. Ruggles of _____ Gap

30. Clockwork _____

31. Snow _____

32. Forever _____

33. Father _____

34. A Study in _____

35. How _____ Was My Valley

69

Mystery Sleuths

All you mystery fans who love to relax by curling up with a good detective story—how well do you know your sleuths? Listed below are 20 detectives whose fame in literature is quite secure. Can you match each one up with his creator, and with the title of the opus in which he stars? You get a point for each correct answer.

A score of 20 shows skill at deduction; 27 means you don't miss a clue; and 35 makes you a private eye.

THE DETECTIVES

1. HERCULE POIROT
2. PHILIP MARLOWE
3. FATHER BROWN
4. NERO WOLFE
5. C. AUGUSTE DUPIN
6. TABARET
7. SAM SPADE
8. SECRET AGENT 007
9. TOMMY HAMBLEDON
10. SHERLOCK HOLMES
11. PERRY MASON
12. CHARLIE CHAN
13. LEW ARCHER
14. PHILO VANCE
15. MIKE HAMMER
16. RODERICK ALLEYN
17. PETER WIMSEY
18. DR. GIDEON FELL
19. ELLERY QUEEN
20. TRAVIS MCGEE

THE AUTHORS	THE BOOKS
A. Edgar Allan Poe	a. *The Roman Hat Mystery*
B. Arthur Conan Doyle	b. *The Maltese Falcon*
C. Earl D. Biggers	c. *Goldfinger*
D. S.S. Van Dine	d. *The Problem of the Green Capsule*
E. Frederic Dannay & Manfred B. Lee	e. *Murders in Rue Morgue*
F. G.K. Chesterton	f. *I, the Jury*
G. Rex Stout	g. *Monsieur Le Coq*
H. Erle Stanley Gardner	h. *Twelve Little Indians*
I. Dashiell Hammett	i. *A Study in Scarlet*
J. Dorothy Sayers	j. *Overture to Death*
K. John Dickson Carr	k. *House Without a Key*
L. Ngaio Marsh	l. *Case of the Velvet Claws*
M. Raymond Chandler	m. *The Canary Murder Case*
N. Nanning Coles	n. *The Nine Tailors*
O. Ross Macdonald	o. *The Moving Target*
P. John D. MacDonald	p. *The Blue Cross*
Q. Mickey Spillane	q. *Three for the Chair*
R. Agatha Christie	r. *The Big Sleep*
S. Jan Fleming	s. *Drink to Yesterday*
T. Emile Gaboriau	t. *A Key to the Suite*

Cut and Dried

Below, you will find listed 56 notorious expressions. Each of these similes is as old as the hills, is worn to a frazzle, and has by this time become as dull as dishwater. If you want proof of just how insidious they are, just see how they sneaked into the previous sentence.

However, this is not a sermon on good rhetoric, but a test of your memory. How many of the following phrases can you complete? Take 1 point off for each one you leave blank or get wrong. Give yourself 2 points for each correct answer.

A score of 55 is fine; 75 is dandy; and 95 is super!

1. As fresh as a _____
2. As brown as a _____
3. As neat as a _____
4. As smart as a _____
5. As right as _____
6. As pleased as _____
7. As vain as a _____
8. As meek as a _____
9. As brave as a _____
10. As stiff as a _____
11. As heavy as _____
12. As light as a _____
13. As fit as a _____
14. As green as _____
15. As black as _____
16. As white as a _____

17. As frisky as a _____
18. As pale as a _____
19. As happy as a _____
20. As simple as _____
21. As hard as _____
22. As limp as a _____
23. As slow as _____
24. As quick as a _____
25. As funny as a _____
26. As sly as a _____
27. As cold as _____
28. As cool as a _____
29. As warm as _____
30. As quiet as a _____
31. As good as _____
32. As playful as a _____

33. As blind as a   _____

34. As fat as a   _____

35. As thin as a   _____

36. As hungry as a   _____

37. As dead as a   _____

38. As clean as a   _____

39. As innocent as a   _____

40. As sweet as   _____

41. As pretty as a   _____

42. As ugly as   _____

43. As stubborn as a   _____

44. As sour as a   _____

45. As pleased as   _____

46. As sober as a   _____

47. As sick as a   _____

48. As clear as   _____

49. As keen as a   _____

50. As busy as a   _____

51. As scarce as   _____

52. As slow as a   _____

53. As sharp as a   _____

54. As deep as the   _____

55. As rare as a   _____

56. As bright as a   _____

Sailors and their Ships

Here is a list of characters all of whom are found afloat when crucial action takes place.

Can you match each character with his ship and with his author? Write the appropriate letters in the blanks. Give yourself one point for each correct answer. Then, identify the book and get two extra points.

A score of 20 is seaworthy; 27 puts you at the helm; and 34 makes you the salt of the sea.

THE SAILORS

1. HUCKLEBERRY FINN   ____   _____

2. RICHARD DANA   ____   _____

3. FLETCHER CHRISTIAN   ____   _____

4. HARVEY CHEYNE   ____   _____

5. WOLF LARSEN &
   HUMPHREY VAN WEYDEN   ____   _____

6. HORATIO HORNBLOWER   ____   _____

7. PHILIP FRANCIS QUEEG   ____   _____

8. JIM HAWKINS   ____   _____

9. JAMES WAIT   ____   _____

10. ISHMAEL   ____   _____

11. CAPTAIN NEMO   ____   _____

12. SANTIAGO   ____   _____

74

THE SHIPS

A. Whaler
B. Schooner
C. Pilgrim's brig
D. Skiff
E. Sealing vessel
F. Raft
G. Freighter
H. Frigate
I. Submarine
J. Fishing ship
K. Armed transport
L. Minesweeper

THE AUTHORS

a. Ernest Hemingway
b. Charles Nordhoff & James Norman Hall
c. C.S. Forester
d. Jack London
e. Jules Verne
f. Herman Wouk
g. Rudyard Kipling
h. Robert Louis Stevenson
i. R.H. Dana
j. Mark Twain
k. Herman Melville
l. Joseph Conrad

By the Numbers

You may sometimes forget your own telephone number, but tucked away in your memory there are undoubtedly some numbers that you may not even realize you know. Try it and see. Dredge up a number in answer to the 35 miscellaneous questions below.

A score of 15 shows a minor interest in trivia; 20 makes you a master of the numbers game; and 30 shows an enviable numerical memory.

1. How many lines are there in a sonnet?   9   12   14

2. How many shots are fired by Mat Dillon at the beginning of Gunsmoke?   1   2   3

3. How many freckles are on puppet Howdy Doody's face?   21   34   48

4. How many signed the Declaration of Independence?   24   48   56

5. How many stitches on a regulation baseball?   50   108   148

6. How many self-portraits did Rembrandt paint?   12   42   62

7. What is the only even prime number?   2   4   6

8. How many years must a person be missing to be declared legally dead?   3   7   10

9. At what temperature does book paper catch fire and burn? (Hint: a Ray Bradbury novel)   168°   451°   682°

10. How many words are there in the King James Bible?   215,726   498,608   773,692

11. How many justices on the U.S. Supreme Court?	9	12	14
12. How many players on a cricket team?	9	11	14
13. In which two years did the United States have three presidents?	1801 1901	1841 1961	1881 1964
14. How many feet high is the basket ring for basketball?	10	12	14
15. How many inches was Scarlett O'Hara's waist?	17	22	27
16. How old is Delta Dawn in the country western song?	21	31	41
17. What portion of an iceberg shows above the water?	⅓	¼	⅑
18. How many players on a hurling team?	9	11	15
19. How many years did Sleeping Beauty sleep?	40	100	150
20. How many bones in the human body?	174	206	342
21. How many pints of blood are there in the body of the average human?	12	18	24
22. How many years does Lincoln mention at the beginning of his Gettysburg Address?	47	87	107
23. How many football players from one team are on the field at one time?	9	11	14
24. How old is Huck Finn in Mark Twain's novel?	9	13	17

25. How many seconds does it take the tape on Mission Impossible to self-destruct?   5   10   30

26. What is the distance in feet between bases in baseball?   60   90   120

27. How many players on a Lacrosse team?   5   8   10

28. How many dimples are there on a golf ball?   336   416   506

29. How many plagues were visited on Egypt when the Pharaoh refused Moses' request to let the Hebrews leave?   10   12   15

30. How many sheets of paper are there in a ream?   250   350   500

31. How many minutes did the movie *Gone With the Wind* run?   90   120   220

32. Bluebeard's last wife, Fatima, was his number   6   7   8

33. King Henry VIII had how many wives in all?   6   7   8

34. How many wives did the Mormon leader, Brigham Young, marry in all?   7   17   27

35. How many years does the Bible tell us Methusaleh lived?   900   909   969

In Sickness and in Health

You may never have to deliver a baby in an emergency, but you are often called upon to use your medical knowledge in less dramatic ways. Below are 12 statements for you to label true or false.

A score of 8 or better makes you a friend in need, indeed.

	TRUE	FALSE
1. To remove an object lodged in one of your nostrils, cover the free passage and exhale strongly.	_____	_____
2. The old saying, "Feed a cold and starve a fever," is medically sound.	_____	_____
3. The higher the fever, the sicker the patient is.	_____	_____
4. A severe stomach pain should be treated with hot compresses.	_____	_____
5. Sickrooms should be kept very warm, in the range of 75 to 80 degrees.	_____	_____
6. During hot weather, it is not advisable to use a fan in a sickroom.	_____	_____
7. Any variation in a person's temperature is a sign of illness.	_____	_____
8. After being opened and used, medicines can be safely stored for future use.	_____	_____
9. If a baby has swallowed a foreign object, turn him upside down by holding his legs up.	_____	_____
10. If a bone is stuck in a person's throat, give him a piece of bread to swallow.	_____	_____
11. To treat a minor burn, pour cold water generously over it.	_____	_____
12. Apply cold compresses to a sprained ankle.	_____	_____

For Bette Davis Fans

Heroines, harridans, harlots, and hags—Bette Davis played every kind of role, and so convincingly that many consider her America's best as well as most versatile film actress.

How much do you know about the woman who has been called America's "First Lady of the Screen?" Below are 22 questions. You have three choices. Check the answer you believe to be correct.

A score of 12 is fine; 15 is admirable; 18 is great; and 21 is Davis-tating.

1. Bette Davis's real name is:
   Bettina Dawes   Ruth Elizabeth Davis   Norma Jean Baker

2. Bette Davis was born in 1908 in:
   Lowell, Massachusetts   Savannah, Georgia
              Hartford, Connecticut

3. Bette Davis studied dance with:
   Isadora Duncan   Martha Graham   Ruth St. Denis

4. Bette's famous line, "What a dump!" comes from what movie?
   Of Human Bondage   *Beyond the Forest*   *Jezebel*

5. Bette's first professional acting experience was with the stock company of a famous movie director. He was:
   Howard Hawks   John Huston   George Cukor

6. Bette Davis was not well known until she gave a brilliant performance as the sluttish Mildred Rogers in *Of Human Bondage*. The movie was based on a novel by:
   Theodore Dreiser   Leslie Howard   Somerset Maugham

7. Bette's co-star in *Mr. Skeffington* was:
   Leslie Howard   Claude Rains   Humphrey Bogart

8. *Jezebel*, one of Davis's best-loved movies, was made in:
   1930   1938   1948

9. Bette played a frumpy Bronx housewife in:
   The Little Foxes   *Juarez*   *The Catered Affair*

10. For 18 years, Bette Davis was under contract to what movie studio?
    United Artists   Paramount Pictures   Warner Brothers Studios

11. Davis made her movie debut in:
    1931   1933   1935

12. Bette played a character named Joyce Heath in:
    Dangerous   *Kid Galahad*   *A Marked Woman*

13. Which historical queen did Bette Davis play, in two different movies?
    Catherine the Great of Russia
    Elizabeth I of England
    Queen Christine of Sweden

14. Bette's co-star in *Whatever Happened to Baby Jane?* was:
    Joan Fontaine   Joan Crawford   Olivia de Havilland

15. Bette's fourth husband was:
    Actor Gary Merrill   Recluse Howard Hughes
                    Bandleader Harmon Nelson

16. "Fasten your seatbelts—it's going to be a bumpy evening," is a line
    spoken by what Davis character?
    Charlotte Vale   Margot Channing   Joyce Heath

17. Bette Davis was the first woman elected president of the Academy of
    Motion Picture Arts and Sciences, in:
    1938   1941   1961

18. Which of the following movies did Bette *not* star in?
    Watch on the Rhine   *The Old Maid*   *Sunset Boulevard*

19. Bette Davis has how many children?
    None   Three   Six

20. Davis played opposite George Arliss in what film?
    The Man Who Came to Dinner   *The Great Lie*
                    The Man Who Played God

21. In *Bad Sister*, Davis's first movie, her male co-star was another tyro.
    His name was:
    Spencer Tracy   Humphrey Bogart   James Stewart

22. Bette Davis began her film career under contract to what studio?
    Warner Brothers   Universal   Columbia

Remember Radio?

These days, everyone watches TV. How well do you remember the days when everyone was tuned in to the radio set?

Below are 25 questions about radio programs. Check the answer you believe to be correct. There are three choices.

A score of 12 beats the band; 16 is a high frequency score, and 20 means you're on the right wave length.

1. What radio soap opera asked the question, "Can this girl from a mining town in the West find happiness as the wife of a wealthy and titled Englishman?"
   Helen Trent   *Hilltop House*   *Our Gal Sunday*

2. Mayor La Trivia was a character on what radio comedy:
   Ma Perkins   *Fibber McGee and Molly*   *Abbott and Costello*

3. *The Fat Man* was a radio series created by:
   Dashiell Hammett   Erle Stanley Gardner   Alfred Hitchcock

4. Ma Perkins's daughters were named:
   Kathleen and Meggin   Janice and Louise   Fay and Evey

5. Jack Benny always gave his age as:
   29   30   39

6. Socrates Mulligan, a character on *Allen's Alley*, was played by:
   Charles Cantor   Fred Allen   Kenny Delmar

7. The last name of Amos on the *Amos 'n' Andy Show* was:
   White   Smith   Jones

8. "Who knows what evil lurks in the hearts of men?" began the radio series:
   Boston Blackie   *The Shadow*   *The Green Hornet*

9. Baby Snooks was a radio character played by:
   Barbra Streisand   Barbara Stanwyk   Fanny Brice

10. The Barbour family, of the series *One Man's Family*, lived in:
    New York City   San Francisco   Oshkosh, Wisconsin

11. *Big Town* was a radio series about a:
    Doctor   Detective   Newspaperman

12. Captain Henry was a character on:
    The Maxwell House Showboat   *Captain Midnight*
                    Chandu the Magician

13. Charlie Chan, the Chinese detective, was originally played on radio
    by:
    Walter Connolly   Walter Pidgeon   J. Carroll Nash

14. Detective Nick Carter's adopted son was named:
    Junior   Nicky   Chick

15. Conelrad (Control of Electromagnetic Radiation), a now obsolete civil
    defense measure, was located where on the radio dial?
    640 and 1240 AM   530 and 1600 AM   700 and 1400 AM

16. The marshall in *Gunsmoke* was named:
    Wyatt Earp   Chester   Matt Dillon

17. *Truth or Consequences* was a:
    Soap opera   Quiz show   Mystery series

18. The host of *Houseparty* was:
    Clifton Fadiman   George Burns   Art Linkletter

19. The radio series dedicated to "The Women of America" was:
    Hilltop House   *Helen Trent*   *Ma Perkins*

20. The sponsor of *Your Hit Parade* was:
    Chesterfield   Lucky Strike   Pall Mall

21. Effie Perine was the secretary of:
    Sam Spade   Perry Mason   Clark Kent

22. The locale of the radio serial *Pepper Young's Family* was:
    Five Points   Elmwood   Fernwood

23. The nickname of Mike Waring was:
    The Shadow   The Falcon   Fang

24. *Flight of the Bumblebee* was the theme song of:
    The Lone Ranger   *The Green Hornet*   *The Shadow*

25. The star and creator of *The Goldbergs* was:
    Arlene McQuade   Gertrude Berg   Marian Jordan

Free-For-All

The 35 statements below have to do with everything and anything, and they add up to absolutely nothing. Can you recognize which of the statements are true and which statements false? Check True or False.

A score of 15 is fine; 20 is super; and 25 is awesome.

	TRUE	FALSE
1. The largest country in the world is China.	___	___
2. Harpo Marx was left-handed.	___	___
3. The skeleton of the earliest horse is estimated to be 45 million years old.	___	___
4. A tatterdemalion is a kind of lizard.	___	___
5. The most populous country in the world is India.	___	___
6. Parker Pyne is a detective invented by Agatha Christie.	___	___
7. Johnny Appleseed's real name was Paul Bunyan.	___	___
8. An oxymoron is a person of low intelligence.	___	___
9. In the movie *Gone With the Wind*, Scarlett O'Hara was played by Janet Leigh.	___	___
10. The average elevation of the United States, except for Alaska and Hawaii, is about 2,500 feet above sea level.	___	___
11. Tagliatelle was the name of a great 19th century ballerina.	___	___
12. Alexander Hamilton was killed in a duel with Benedict Arnold.	___	___
13. Mali is a country in Central America.	___	___
14. The comic strip *Alley Oop* was created by V.T. Hamlin.	___	___
15. A numismatist is a person who studies insects.	___	___

16. The modern mailbox was invented by novelist Anthony Trollope. ___ ___

17. *Volpone* is a play by William Shakespeare. ___ ___

18. Aluminum is a good conductor of heat. ___ ___

19. The largest denomination of paper money printed in the United States today is the hundred dollar bill. ___ ___

20. The first New York newspaper was the *New York Times*. ___ ___

21. Something that is nugatory is worth its weight in gold. ___ ___

22. The trackless trolley originated in Los Angeles. ___ ___

23. Brass is an alloy of copper. ___ ___

24. Honoré de Balzac wrote 97 novels. ___ ___

25. The vacuum cleaner was invented by James Thurber. ___ ___

26. The native habitat of the griffin is New Zealand. ___ ___

27. The highest mountain is Everest. ___ ___

28. King Solomon was the son of David and Bathsheba. ___ ___

29. If you received your change in escudos, you would probably be in Peru. ___ ___

30. When it is noon in New York (during Daylight Saving Time), it is 6:00 A.M. in Cairo. ___ ___

31. The capital of California is San Francisco. ___ ___

32. The Magna Carta was signed in 1066. ___ ___

33. Franklin D. Roosevelt's first Vice-President was John N. Garner. ___ ___

34. The novel *For Whom the Bell Tolls* was written by Ernest Hemingway. ___ ___

35. The movie *All About Eve* was directed by John Huston. ___ ___

Hoop-La!

How much do you know about basketball? Below are 32 questions about America's biggest sport. See how many answers you know. You have three choices. Check the answer you believe is correct.

A score of 15 is good; 21 is superb; and 27 nets you a championship rating.

1. The longest collegiate basketball shot, estimated at 55 feet by Madison Square Garden officials, was made on March 14, 1946, by a 5'10" player named Ernie Calverley. He was playing for:
   Rhode Island State   Oklahoma Aggies   St. John

2. Who was the highest professional scorer in history?
   Larry Costello   Bob Petit   Wilt Chamberlain

3. The originator of modern basketball was:
   Abner Doubleday   Bill Tilden   James Naismith

4. Kareem Abdul-Jabbar was born with the name:
   Tom Chamberlain   Ferdinand Lewis Alcindor   Andy Wright

5. What team did Bill Russell play on?
   Los Angeles Lakers   Boston Celtics   New York Knickerbockers

6. A basketball attendance record was set in 1951, at Olympic Stadium in West Berlin, Germany. How many fans appeared to watch the Harlem Globetrotters' high jinks?
   50,000   75,000   100,000

7. The tallest basketball player in the history of the game was:
   Bob Lanier of Detroit   Mu Tieh-Chu of China
   George Mikan of Minneapolis

8. The driving genius of the original Celtics was:
   Nat Holman   Dutch Leonard   James Naismith

9. Approximately how many high school basketball teams are there in America?
   10,000   20,000   50,000

10. The first country outside the United States to adopt basketball was:
    England   China   Canada

11. Worldwide, how does basketball rank among sports as a popular spectator sport:
    First   Third   Fifth

12. The only college team to win both the NCAA and the NIT championships in the same year was:
    New York City College   UCLA   New York University

13. Wilt Chamberlain's nickname is:
    Runty   The Stilt   Mr. Basketball

14. Women's basketball began in the:
    1840s   1890s   1920s

15. There are how many teams in the four divisions of the NBA?
    15   22   32

16. Who was the best professional foul shooter ever?
    Julius Erving   Oscar Robertson   Bill Sharman

17. Goaltending refers to:
    Interference with the ball on its final arch toward the basket
    Guarding the best forward on the opposite team
    Staying in your own court, so when a teammate gets the ball, he
        can throw it to you

18. The first intercollegiate basketball game, with seven men per team, was played in 1896. The teams were:
    Harvard and Princeton   Wesleyan and Yale
             University of Chicago and UCLA

19. Professional basketball games are played in four quarters. Each quarter lasts how many minutes?
    12   20   35

20. Basketball has been part of the Olympic Games since:
    1910   1936   1945

21. In basketball, it is illegal to:
    Dribble the ball   Roll the ball   Run holding the ball

22. What is the greatest number of points ever scored by a single player in one game:

    60   80   100

23. The time limit for an offensive team to make a shot is:

    15 seconds   24 seconds   38 seconds

24. The lowest free-throw percentage for the 1976-77 season was set by center Kim Hughes of the New Jersey Jets. His percentage was:

    .275   .325   .395

25. The men's basketball gold medal in the 1976 summer Olympics was won by what country?

    U.S.S.R.   Canada   U.S.

26. In 1978, the N.B.A. Most Valuable Player was:

    George Gervin   Bill Walton   David Thompson

27. George McGinnis left what University to sign up with the Pacers?

    Indiana   UCLA   Texas

28. The N.B.A. player with the longest service is:

    John Kerr   Wilt Chamberlain   John Havlicek

29. The first black man to lead a major league team was:

    Bill Russell   Willis Reed   Kareem Abdul-Jabber

30. The women's championship was won five consecutive times by the team from:

    United States   U.S.S.R.   Brazil

31. Dave Cowens distinguished himself playing:

    Center   Guard   Forward

32. In 1956, when Bill Russell first signed with the Boston Celtics, his salary for that year was:

    $10,000 $20,000 $40,000

Common Cognomens

Below you will find a list of 20 last names. These surnames are all so common that each one of them takes up at least a full page in the New York City telephone directory.

But do you know which 10 of these are the most common last names in the United States? Check the 10 names which you believe to be the most common.

Now rank the names from one to ten, in order of frequency. The name you believe to be the most common would be number one, the second most common, number two, etc.

Check your list against the answers, and award yourself two points for every correct name. Subtract one point for every incorrect answer. Now, additionally, you score two free points for every name you have placed in the right order of frequency.

A total score of 9 is good; 14 is fine; and 20 says you are either very bright or very lucky.

1. White		11. Schwartz
2. Smith		12. Singer
3. Walker		13. Rivera
4. Morris		14. Davis
5. Johnson		15. Anderson
6. Williams		16. Brown
7. Jones		17. Scott
8. Edwards		18. Miller
9. Thompson		19. Roberts
10. Wilson		20. Marshall

Grab Bag

In this quiz, we have gathered together 23 questions pertaining to just about anything you can imagine. There was absolutely no method to our madness.

Check the answer you deem correct. Give yourself one point for each correct answer. A score of ten does credit to your capacity for retaining useless information; 15 is a track record to be proud of; and 20 earns you the triviata trophy of the year.

1. A cretin is:
   A person of low intelligence   A small wildflower
              An inhabitant of one of the Greek islands

2. The highest city in the world is:
   Lhasa, Tibet   Bogota, Columbia   Addis Ababa, Ethiopia

3. Who said, *"Hope springs eternal in the human breast?"*
   William Shakespeare   Alexander Pope   Arthur Godfrey

4. Venison is the meat of a:
   Buffalo   Yak   Deer

5. The country with the lowest life expectancy is:
   Guinea, Africa   Chad, Africa   Nigeria, Africa

6. A marimba is a:
   Cuban dance   Guatemalan stew
            Musical instrument which resembles a xylophone

7. The hottest city in the world is:
   Khartoum, Sudan   Timbuktu, Mali   Niamey, Nigeria

8. Atavism is:
   The study of birds   Very limited eyesight
            Reversion to characteristics in one's remote ancestors

9. "The Little Brown Wren" was the nickname of which Hollywood film star?
   Bette Davis   Olivia de Havilland   Natalie Wood

10. Someone referred to as Brobdingnagian is likely to be:
    Gigantic   A native of a town in Siberia   Puppet-like

11. A trapezoid is:
    A quadrilateral rectangle having only two sides parallel
    A snare used to catch especially wild animals
    An order of monks, which still flourishes in French-speaking Switzerland

12. *Song of Myself* is a long poem by:
    William Wordsworth   Walt Whitman
           Henry Wadsworth Longfellow

13. The greatest harness-racing horse that ever lived was:
    Dancer's Image   Goldsmith Maid   My Friend, Flicka

14. Comestibles are:
    Things which catch fire easily   Eatables
           Rubbers made of gutta percha and tin

15. The fastest hockey skater, Bobby Hull, has been timed at:
    19.7 mph   29.7 mph   49.7 mph

16. The Rosetta Stone is in:
    The British Museum   Luxor, Egypt   Tiffany's, New York

17. The opera *Il Trovatore* was written by:
    Arturo Toscanini   Gaetano Donizetti   Giuseppe Verdi

18. Mickey Wright is a great:
    Jockey   Golfer   Rock singer

19. New South Wales is located in:
    The British Isles   Australia   The Orkney Islands

20. The first person in history to swim the English Channel was:
    Matthew Webb   Allerondro Scalini   Johnny Weissmuller

21. Apiphobia is a fear of:
    Enclosed spaces   Cats   Bees

22. The Garden State is:
    California   Florida   New Jersey

23. The densest planet in the universe is:
    Venus   Jupiter   Earth

How To Solve Threezies

You are given a sequence of three letters. List all the words you can think of which contain these three letters *in exact sequence*.

The sequence may seem quite unlikely. For example, the sequence of letters R R H at first sight might seem completely hopeless, yet with a little thought you might come up with the words *catarrh* and *myrrh*. If the given three letters were M B S, you might find that out of this strange sequence you can form the words *numbskull* and *tombstone*.

The rules of the game are very simple. You may use only one form of a word. For example, if the threezie were N D L, a proper answer would be HANDLE. But then you couldn't use the words HANDLES, HANDLED, or HANDLING, since all these words are forms of the same root. However, where two words have a completely different usage, then they may both be used even though the roots are similar. Thus, since FOND is an adjective and FONDLE is a verb, you could score with the words FOND, or FONDLY, and also with the word FONDLE.

Proper names are off limits; hyphenated words are not allowed.

A C O

There are at least 18 words that contain the letter sequence ACO. How many can you list?

A score of 9 is fine; 13 or more is a coveted score.

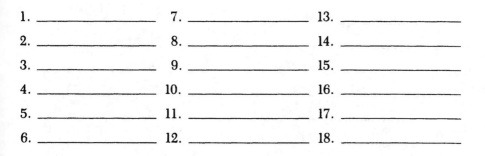

1. _____   7. _____   13. _____

2. _____   8. _____   14. _____

3. _____   9. _____   15. _____

4. _____   10. _____   16. _____

5. _____   11. _____   17. _____

6. _____   12. _____   18. _____

A R N

At least 25 words may be found with the letter sequence ARN. How many can you list?

A score of 12 is decent; 17 or more is far nicer.

1. _____   9. _____   18. _____

2. _____   10. _____   19. _____

3. _____   11. _____   20. _____

4. _____   12. _____   21. _____

5. _____   13. _____   22. _____

6. _____   14. _____   23. _____

7. _____   15. _____   24. _____

8. _____   16. _____   25. _____

17. _____

N C O

There are at least 53 words which contain the letter sequence N C O. How many can you find? List them below.

A score of 25 is good; 35 is excellent; and 45 rates a medal.

1. _____	19. _____	36. _____
2. _____	20. _____	37. _____
3. _____	21. _____	38. _____
4. _____	22. _____	39. _____
5. _____	23. _____	40. _____
6. _____	24 _____	41. _____
7. _____	25. _____	42. _____
8. _____	26. _____	43. _____
9. _____	27. _____	44. _____
10. _____	28. _____	45. _____
11. _____	29. _____	46. _____
12. _____	30. _____	47. _____
13. _____	31. _____	48. _____
14. _____	32. _____	49. _____
15. _____	33. _____	50. _____
16. _____	34. _____	51. _____
17. _____	35. _____	52. _____
18. _____		53. _____

(DIRECTIONS FOR SOLVING THREEZIES ARE ON PAGE 92)

A B R

At least 18 words contain the letter sequence ABR. How many can you find?

A score of 9 is good; 13 is a bright score, indeed.

1. _____   7. _____   13. _____
2. _____   8. _____   14. _____
3. _____   9. _____   15. _____
4. _____   10. _____   16. _____
5. _____   11. _____   17. _____
6. _____   12. _____   18. _____

I D A

There are at least 24 words which contain the letter sequence I D A. How many can you find? List them below.

A score of 13 is good; 17 is excellent; and 20 puts you with the experts.

1. _____   9. _____   17. _____
2. _____   10. _____   18. _____
3. _____   11. _____   19. _____
4. _____   12. _____   20. _____
5. _____   13. _____   21. _____
6. _____   14. _____   22. _____
7. _____   15. _____   23. _____
8. _____   16. _____   24. _____

(DIRECTIONS FOR SOLVING THREEZIES ARE ON PAGE 92)

A D R

We found 28 words that contain the sequence ADR. How many can you list? A score of 14 is adequate; 21 is a darned good score.

1. _____   10. _____   20. _____
2. _____   11. _____   21. _____
3. _____   12. _____   22. _____
4. _____   13. _____   23. _____
5. _____   14. _____   24. _____
6. _____   15. _____   25. _____
7. _____   16. _____   26. _____
8. _____   17. _____   27. _____
9. _____   18. _____   28. _____
                        19. _____

N Q U

There are at least 17 words with the letter sequence NQU. A score of 8 should not make you anxious; 13 or more ranks you way up there.

1. _____   7. _____   12. _____
2. _____   8. _____   13. _____
3. _____   9. _____   14. _____
4. _____   10. _____   15. _____
5. _____   11. _____   16. _____
6. _____   17. _____

(DIRECTIONS FOR SOLVING THREEZIES ARE ON PAGE 92)

O L A

At least 33 words may be found that contain the letter sequence OLA. A score of 15 is worth an olé; 25 or more deserves lavish praise.

1. _____
2. _____
3. _____
4. _____
5. _____
6. _____
7. _____
8. _____
9. _____
10. _____
11. _____

12. _____
13. _____
14. _____
15. _____
16. _____
17. _____
18. _____
19. _____
20. _____
21. _____
22. _____

23. _____
24. _____
25. _____
26. _____
27. _____
28. _____
29. _____
30. _____
31. _____
32. _____
33. _____

L B A

At least 8 words can be found with the letter sequence LBA. How many can you list? A score of 4 or more means you're a real badinage pro.

1. _____
2. _____
3. _____

4. _____
5. _____

6. _____
7. _____
8. _____

(DIRECTIONS FOR SOLVING THREEZIES ARE ON PAGE 92)

E M O

There are at least 28 words which contain the letter sequence EMO. How many can you find? List them below.

A score of 14 is good; 20 is wonderful; and 23 is magnificent.

1. _____
2. _____
3. _____
4. _____
5. _____
6. _____
7. _____
8. _____
9. _____

10. _____
11. _____
12. _____
13. _____
14. _____
15. _____
16. _____
17. _____
18. _____
19. _____

20. _____
21. _____
22. _____
23. _____
24. _____
25. _____
26. _____
27. _____
28. _____

R H O

There are at least nine words with the letter sequence R H O.

If you find five or more, that's superb.

1._____
2._____
3._____

4._____
5._____
6._____

7._____
8._____
9._____

E P T

There are at least 30 words which contain the letter sequence EPT. How many can you find? List them below.

A score of 16 is pretty good; 19 is superior; and 22 or more is outstanding.

1. _____   11. _____   21. _____

2. _____   12. _____   22. _____

3. _____   13. _____   23. _____

4. _____   14. _____   24. _____

5. _____   15. _____   25. _____

6. _____   16. _____   26. _____

7. _____   17. _____   27. _____

8. _____   18. _____   28. _____

9. _____   19. _____   29. _____

10. _____   20. _____   30. _____

L B O

We have listed 12 words with the letter sequence L B O.
   Finding six or more is just fine.

1. _____   5. _____   9. _____

2. _____   6. _____   10. _____

3. _____   7. _____   11. _____

4. _____   8. _____   12. _____

(DIRECTIONS FOR SOLVING THREEZIES ARE ON PAGE 92)

A G O

We found 30 words that contain the letter sequence AGO. How many can you list?

A score of 15 is a good one; 22 or more means you've a good head for words.

1. _____	10. _____	21. _____
2. _____	11. _____	22. _____
3. _____	12. _____	23. _____
4. _____	13. _____	24. _____
5. _____	14. _____	25. _____
6. _____	15. _____	26. _____
7. _____	16. _____	27. _____
8. _____	17. _____	28. _____
9. _____	18. _____	29. _____
10. _____	20. _____	30. _____

R D U

We list a mere six words that contain the letter sequence R D U. How many can you identify?

Anything over three is commendable.

1._____	3._____	5._____
2._____	4._____	6._____

(DIRECTIONS FOR SOLVING THREEZIES ARE ON PAGE 92)

HLO

There are at least 8 words which contain the letter sequence H L O. How many can you find? List them below.

A score of 4 is very good; 6 is exceptional; and 7 is really outstanding.

1. _____ 4. _____ 6. _____

2. _____ 5. _____ 7. _____

3. _____   8. _____

(DIRECTIONS FOR SOLVING THREEZIES ARE ON PAGE 92)

RLO

There are at least 25 words that contain the letter sequence R L O. If you list 12, that's fairly good; 18 or more is really super.

1. _____   9. _____   18. _____

2. _____   10. _____ 19. _____

3. _____   11. _____ 20. _____

4. _____   12. _____ 21. _____

5. _____   13. _____ 22. _____

6. _____   14. _____ 23. _____

7. _____   15. _____ 24. _____

8. _____   16. _____ 25. _____

                     17. _____

FTY

At least 9 words may be listed that contain the letter sequence F T Y. How many can you find?

A score of 5 or more is admirable.

1. _____   4. _____   7. _____

2. _____   5. _____   8. _____

3. _____   6. _____   9. _____

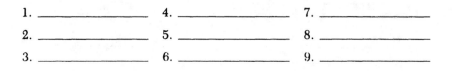

(DIRECTIONS FOR SOLVING THREEZIES ARE ON PAGE 92)

LTR

We found 12 words with the letter sequence L T R. How many can you list?

A score of 7 or more shows you're well-lettered.

1. _____   5. _____   9. _____

2. _____   6. _____   10. _____

3. _____   7. _____   11. _____

4. _____   8. _____   12. _____

ABA

There are at least 24 words with the letter sequence A B A. How many can you come up with?

A score of 12 shows you're capable; 18 is well above average.

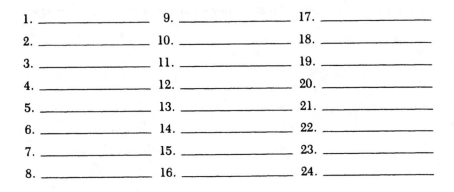

1. _____   9. _____   17. _____

2. _____   10. _____   18. _____

3. _____   11. _____   19. _____

4. _____   12. _____   20. _____

5. _____   13. _____   21. _____

6. _____   14. _____   22. _____

7. _____   15. _____   23. _____

8. _____   16. _____   24. _____

(DIRECTIONS FOR SOLVING THREEZIES ARE ON PAGE 92)

GNA

There are at least 20 words that contain the letter sequence G N A. How many can you list?

A score of 10 is nice; 15 or more is magnificent.

1. _____
2. _____
3. _____
4. _____
5. _____
6. _____
7. _____
8. _____
9. _____
10. _____
11. _____
12. _____
13. _____
14. _____
15. _____
16. _____
17. _____
18. _____
19. _____
20. _____

MNA

We list only 10 words with the letter sequence M N A. Can you top this?

A score of 5 or more is commendable.

1. _____
2. _____
3. _____
4. _____
5. _____
6. _____
7. _____
8. _____
9. _____
10. _____

ERB

We found 25 words with the letter sequence E R B. How many can you list?

A score of 12 is fair; 17 or more is super.

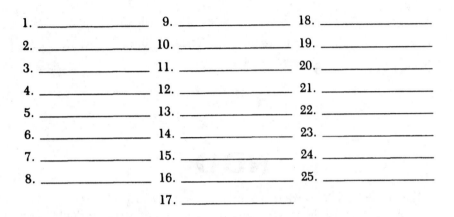

1. _____   9. _____   18. _____
2. _____   10. _____   19. _____
3. _____   11. _____   20. _____
4. _____   12. _____   21. _____
5. _____   13. _____   22. _____
6. _____   14. _____   23. _____
7. _____   15. _____   24. _____
8. _____   16. _____   25. _____
                       17. _____

LRY

We found only 7 words with the letter sequence L R Y. How many can you list?

A score of 4 or more shows you really tried.

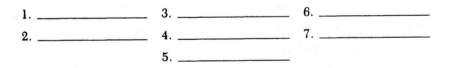

1. _____   3. _____   6. _____
2. _____   4. _____   7. _____
                        5. _____

(DIRECTIONS FOR SOLVING THREEZIES ARE ON PAGE 92)

UBL

There are at least 12 words that contain the letter sequence U B L. How many can you find? List them below.

A score of 7 is very good; 9 is superior; and 11 is stupendous.

1. _____   5. _____   9. _____
2. _____   6. _____   10. _____
3. _____   7. _____   11. _____
4. _____   8. _____   12. _____

NDO

There are at least 25 words that contain the letter sequence N D O.

A score of 14 shows you can do; 20 or more leaves no doubt about your verbal skill.

1. _____   9. _____   18. _____
2. _____   10. _____   19. _____
3. _____   11. _____   20. _____
4. _____   12. _____   21. _____
5. _____   13. _____   22. _____
6. _____   14. _____   23. _____
7. _____   15. _____   24. _____
8. _____   16. _____   25. _____
                     17. _____

(DIRECTIONS FOR SOLVING THREEZIES ARE ON PAGE 92)

How to Solve
Word Search Puzzles

You are given a large jumble of letters and a list of words; the object is to find these words in the block of letters. The words may appear left-to-right, right-to-left, down a column, up a column, or even diagonally.

In each case, the first word on the list is located for you.

Happy hunting!

Rounding Curves

As you can see from the example, there is a special angle to this puzzle! Each of the 23 words buried in the circle may start out or end up in a straightforward way, but somewhere along the line it may take a bend. So, search vertically, horizontally, diagonally, backwards and forwards, as usual, but be sure to find the angle. Keep at it and don't let the curves throw you.

If you can ferret out all the words in 25 minutes or less, you've watched a lot of tennis matches.

AIRPLANE	DELICACY	MECHANIC
APPROACH	DIRECTLY	MIDNIGHT
ARKANSAS	ELECTRON	OINTMENT
CANADIAN	ELEPHANT	PARENTAL
CHEMICAL	FAVORITE	PARLANCE
CHESTNUT	INTRIGUE	PHONETIC
CHICKPEA	MANDOLIN	SKIRMISH
CHIPMUNK		STRAIGHT

(DIRECTIONS FOR SOLVING WORD SEARCHES ARE ON PAGE 107)

```
            E  N  A  B  L  L
         O  M  U  N  K  O  A  A  L  R
      N  P  A  R  E  N  T  S  E  H  C  C
   M  I  S  A  S  A  S  N  T  N  E  M  T  M
   I  H  S  I  N  G  N  R  U  S  T  Y  G  S  N  H
   C  O  R  T  N  A  H  P  T  U  L  L  T  C  R  I
O  Y  E  P  N  K  M  E  E  B  T  O  R  I  T  E  C  O
S  C  C  L  R  A  U  L  L  C  V  A  K  P  E  A  H  P
P  A  N  A  V  D  I  R  E  A  I  T  C  B  D  E  E  H
M  C  A  N  W  M  N  D  F  K  G  M  I  E  F  I  M  O
E  I  L  E  D  I  T  I  A  L  H  E  H  L  A  C  I  N
R  R  R  A  P  D  R  G  N  J  T  C  C  T  C  I  T  E
   T  H  G  I  N  I  I  A  A  A  H  A  N  I  C  E
   I  R  S  S  G  H  A  C  O  S  T  I  T  U  L  S
      H  Q  U  A  P  P  R  I  R  L  V  W  E  E
         E  S  K  I  R  M  N  O  R  T  C  V
         D  E  M  A  N  D  D  X  G  L
            T  Z  I  S  Y  Y
```

The Wild West

Here's your chance to be a dude rancher and explore the frontier from the comfort of your living room. Get on your imaginary hoss and don't stop until you have rounded up all 51 words listed below. Travel vertically, horizontally, diagonally, and backwards and forwards.

If you complete your mission in 15 minutes or less, you must have a blazing saddle.

BOOTS	FORT	LEAD
BOWIE KNIFE	GOLD LUST	LOST
BREW	GO WEST	MULES
BUFFALO	GRUB	PLOW
CODE	GUST	PONY EXPRESS
COLT	HATS	PRAIRIE
COVERED WAGON	HORSES	RIGS
DOWN	HUNT	RIFLE
DUST	INDIAN	RUNS
FEARS	IRONS	SADDLE
FIGHTING	JESSE JAMES	SANTE FE
FIRES	JOHN WAYNE	SHELLS
FIST	JOIN	SHOOTING

(DIRECTIONS FOR SOLVING WORD SEARCHES ARE ON PAGE 107)

```
T  R  O  O  P  A  M  U  L  E  S  A  D  D  L  E  V  C
S  L  L  E  H  S  B  R  E  W  T  H  U  T  R  E  K  O
K  E  O  H  U  N  T  Y  S  N  S  I  O  U  X  B  F  V
I  I  S  G  B  U  F  F  A  L  O  C  D  R  E  F  I  E
N  R  T  H  T  R  F  I  G  H  T  I  N  G  S  I  R  R
S  I  S  B  R  E  D  O  C  J  K  R  I  F  L  E  E  E
L  A  U  D  A  N  L  L  U  B  G  N  I  T  T  I  S  D
P  R  G  O  I  N  M  J  O (B  O  O  T  S) T  W  H  W
G  P  R  W  N  L  S  G  O  L  D  L  U  S  T  O  O  A
N  L  X  N  I  T  V  W  V  H  I  R  O  N  S  N  O  G
I  O  A  A  L  L  I  E  T  F  N  F  O  R  T  D  T  O
B  W  R  O  H  E  I  S  G  G  O  W  E  S  T  E  I  N
S  T  C  E  K  A  U  R  I  G  S  L  A  M  R  R  N  S
S  S  F  N  B  D  C  D  T  E  N  T  S  Y  S  O  G  P
O  I  I  G  K  S  A  N  T  A  F  E  T  N  N  I  O  J
T  F  E  A  R  S  L  P  O  N  Y  E  X  P  R  E  S  S
E  I  G  S  T  A  G  E  C  O  A  C  H  A  T  S  B  C
A  F  H  J  E  S  S  E  J  A  M  E  S  E  T  R  A  P
```

SIOUX	**TENTS**	**TRAP**
SITTING BULL	**TOSS BIN**	**TREK**
SKINS	**TRAIL**	**TROOP**
STAGECOACH	**TRAIN**	**WONDER**

Ample Test Of Nerves

Each of the 40 words listed below contains either the letters AMP or the letters NER. That clue should help you locate them all in the square. Search up, down, across, on the angle, and backwards and forwards.

If you can circle all the words in 12 minutes, that's a fine exAMPle of eNERgy.

ABNER	HAMPER	REVAMP
AMPHETAMINE	INERT	SAMPLE
AMPHIBIOUS	INNER	SCAMPER
AMPLE	KRONER	SCANNER
AMPUTATION	LAMPOON	SHAMPOO
BONER	LONER	SHATNER
BURNER	MANNERS	SHINER
CAMPER	MINER	STAMP
CORNER	MINERS	STAMPEDE
CRAMP	NERD	TAMPER
DAMPEN	NERO	TAMPON
DINNER	NERVOUS	TRAMP
ENERGY	PAMPER	TRAMPOLINE
	PARTNER	

(DIRECTIONS FOR SOLVING WORD SEARCHES ARE ON PAGE 107)

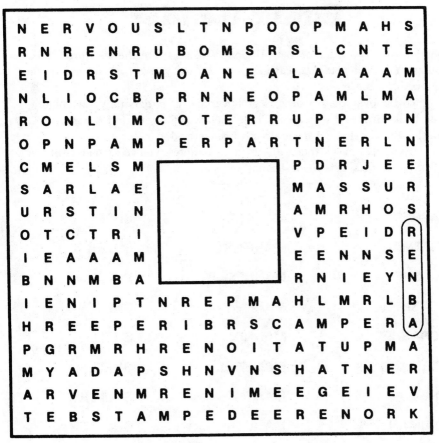

```
N E R V O U S L T N P O O P M A H S
R N R E N R U B O M S R S L C N T E
E I D R S T M O A N E A L A A A A M
N L I O C B P R N N E O P A M L M A
R O N L I M C O T E R R U P P P P N
O P N P A M P E R P A R T N E R L N
C M E L S M           P D R J E E
S A R L A E           M A S S U R
U R S T I N           A M R H O S
O T C T R I           V P E I D R
I E A A A M           E E N N S E
B N N M B A           R N I E Y N
I E N I P T N R E P M A H L M R L B
H R E E P E R I B R S C A M P E R A
P G R M R H R E N O I T A T U P M A
M Y A D A P S H N V N S H A T N E R
A R V E N M R E N I M E E G E I E V
T E B S T A M P E D E E R E N O R K
```

113

Either Gender

Hidden in the word square on the opposite page are the 40 words listed below. You will note that each of these buried words contains either the letters SGE or the letters MAN.

To discover these words, search vertically, horizontally, diagonally, and backwards and forwards. Circle each word as you find it and cross it off the list. The first word has already been circled.

If you can check them all out in 15 minutes, you've earned a SHErry; 10 minutes or less gets you a MANhattan.

ASHES	MANGLE	SHEEP
BATMAN	MANIFEST	SHEER
BUSHEL	MANNEQUIN	SHEIK
CASHEW	MANNER	SHELF
CRASHER	MANNIX	SHELL
DEMAND	MANSFIELD	SHELLAC
HE-MAN	MANTLE	SHELLEY
HUMAN	MANUAL	SHELTER
KOSHER	ROMAN	SHENANIGANS
LASHES	ROMANTIC	SHERATON
LE MANS	RUSHED	SHERIFF
MANDATE	SAMANTHA	SHERLOCK
MANDOLIN	SEAMAN	WOMAN
	SHED	

(DIRECTIONS FOR SOLVING WORD SEARCHES ARE ON PAGE 107)

```
F E R D W L S H E R I F F E S L E N
S H E O K C O L R E H S L H L S C O
S H M N S H A C M E N T E E M A N R
S A M O T U A W R M N L H O L R I O
N M U T N O N I E A F S M L E H U M
N A R A L A O I M H S H E N I U M A
B N M R M S H E R I S H N R O M A N
B D L E I F S N A M S A E O M A N T
T A H H U M A N T N M R C R K N N I
S T T S V F E M A N N E Q U I N I C
A E W M M A N G L E Y O R C E C X R
H S C E A L I S N A M E L S H E R U
T C A M A N I F E S T K P A S E H S
N H S O A M A N I L V R O E S E P H
A M H N Y E L L E H S E H S E H L E
M S E A M A N H D N A M E D H H E D
A H S O B U S H E L P A N A M E S S
S N S H E E R N I L O D N A M P R O
```

115

Zigzag

Up, down, and around go the paths of this maze. Be careful not to zig when you should zag, and you'll find the route to the bottom soon enough.

A 5-minute journey is fair; 4 minutes is an excellent time; and a solution in 2 minutes or less is amazing!

117

Persian Script

These thick and thin curves may remind you of Persian writing, but they'll certainly spell trouble before you find your way through to the bottom.

A solution in 10 minutes is so-so; 8 minutes is much better; and 6 minutes or less is remarkable.

119

City Blocks

This perplexing puzzler should be enough to send even the most clear-eyed city dweller back to the country.

If escape from this cityscape take you more than 15 minutes, you're in the woods; and if you get out in 12 minutes, you're on the right road. If you are free in 10 minutes or less—you must be a city slicker.

121

Math Signs

The basic math signs haven't changed, even with the "New Math."

Pass through this maze and at least one of the signs and out the bottom in 12 minutes and you've passed; in 8 minutes, you've done yourself proud; and a journey of 5 minutes or less earns an honors grade.

123

Third Dimension

The third dimension is depth, and you'll find yourself in deep trouble before you can steer a course through this jumble of objects. If you're home free in 12 minutes, that's mediocre; 10 minutes is good; and 8 minutes or less is sensational.

124

125

Tiptoe

There are no tulips to tiptoe through in this garden, but there are leaves and flowers galore. A 15-minute trip is only a garden-variety feat; 11 minutes smells sweeter; and 9 minutes or less shows a fertile mind.

127

Six Tricks

Start at the top, move from one to six in order, and exit at the bottom. This over-and-under puzzle requires that *no path be followed more than once.* Twenty-two minutes is maximum for this one; 18 minutes is quite good; and a solution in 15 minutes or less adds up to quite a trick.

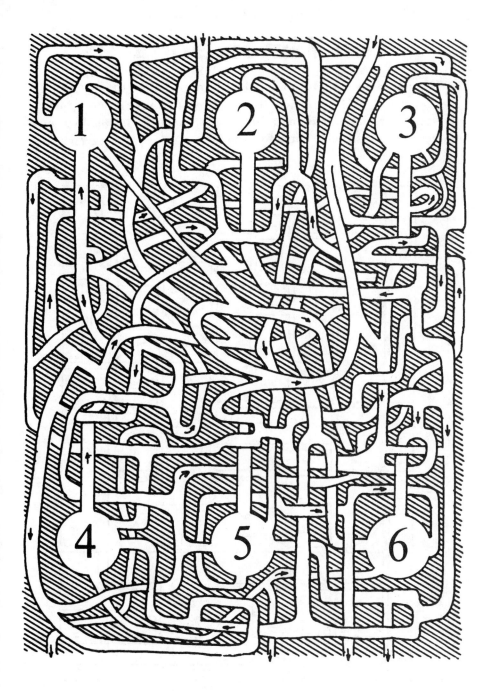

Ten Times Square

Here's a city map with 10 plazas. Traffic must follow the arrows in the plazas, as well as in the side streets. If your journey home takes 15 minutes, you're late for dinner; 10 minutes, you're right on time; and 7 minutes or less, you've got time to spare.

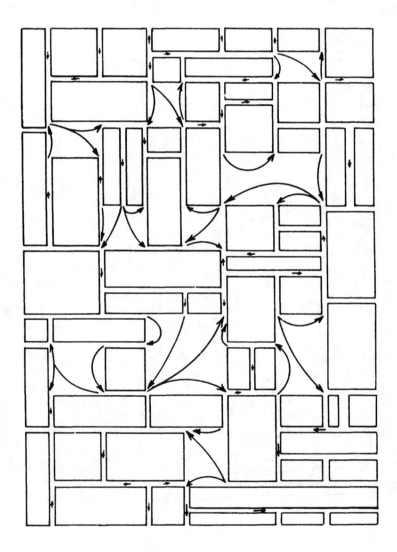

How to Play Scramble

The aim of this game is to figure out the key word, which appears at the bottom of the puzzle. To do this, you are given several clues. The cartoon provides you with one clue to the key word. And the scrambles provide another clue.

To figure out the scrambles, fill in the word for each definition. The boxes tell you how many letters are in each word that is defined.

You will not that some of the boxes are shaded. When you have filled in all the definitions, pick out the letters in the shaded boxes. This is the scramble. Rearrange the letters until they form a word. This is the key word. It corresponds to the word in the cartoon clue. Write this word in the boxes at the bottom of the puzzle.

Scramble No. 1

□○□□
1. To understand; be acquainted with

□○□□
2. To choose; a tooth cleaner; a tool

□□○
3. A writing implement

□○□□□□
4. Assault

□○□□
5. A money institution

□□○
6. A nocturnal animal; a baseball implement

□□○
7. Maker of honey

□○□□□
8. Shorthand writing

□○□□
9. A flower with thorns

A 9-LETTER WORD
THAT'S A GREAT
HEARING AID.

SOLUTION: □□□□□□□□□

(DIRECTIONS FOR SOLVING SCRAMBLES ARE ON PAGE 131)

Scramble No. 2

1. Glue

A 5-LETTER WORD MADE BY LOAFERS, WHO IN THIS WAY EARN IT.

2. A hippy home; a tablet of writing paper

3. A small wagon

4. A hut generally made of logs

5. A color; a communist

SOLUTION:

Scramble No. 3

1. Finger jewelry

2. A living teddy bear from Asia

3. A serious play

4. Lighthearted teasing or joking

5. A close friend

THE BEST THING TO START THE DAY WRONG.

SOLUTION:

(DIRECTIONS FOR SOLVING SCRAMBLES ARE ON PAGE 131)

Scramble No. 4

1. Chemical used as an anesthetic

2. Peel of an orange

3. Stone of peach or plum; a deep hole

4. A purple fruit

5. Used, with a fork, for eating

6. Where one puts the dirty dishes; to go under

7. To pierce with a knife or dagger

IT'S A 7-LETTER WORD AND YOU MAY BE STUCK WITH IT.

SOLUTION: ☐☐☐☐☐☐☐

(DIRECTIONS FOR SOLVING SCRAMBLES ARE ON PAGE 131)

Crossword Puzzle No. 1

1. Good moods
4. Not barefoot
8. Extraterrestrial
13. Seines
15. Lieutenant
16. Miss Lavin
17. Pressed
19. Jewelry stone
21. Scottish cap
22. Trolley
23. Actor Taylor
24. "____ into my parlor..."
25. Swords
28. Cloth made from bark
30. Bath in Baden Baden
32. Sends out
34. Picture
38. For example (Latin abbr.)
39. Actor's part
40. Pie filling
41. Greek war god
44. Related to pitch
46. Espies

47. Originate
49. Tied
51. Per ____
52. Twilled fabric
53. Cubic measure
54. Word with quill or fountain
55. Get better
57. Fixed gaze
59. Homestead
62. Ladle
64. Frees
66. Sea eagle
67. Hitched
68. Avoid
70. *Jacques Brel Is ____ and Well...* (Off-Broadway musical)
72. Relaxation
74. Eagerness
75. Warm
76. Late comedian Laurel
77. Jeanne d'Arc, e.g. (abbr.)

1. Prefix meaning one
2. Saucy
3. Preserved
4. Morose
5. 50th state (abbr.)
6. Smell

7. Stations
8. "____ in a day's work"
9. Year in Claudius' reign
10. Very involved with
11. Mellow Dutch cheese
12. Title

136

14. Break
18. Asian ruler (variant)
20. Nabokov title
24. Bivouacs
26. Express feeling
27. Farm storehouse
29. Fruit seed
30. "Baubles, Bangles and ____"
    (Kismet)
31. Reach accord
33. Belief
35. Malt beverage
36. Gander's girlfriends
37. German iron center
40. Vigilant
42. Make a mistake
43. Vision
45. Hails!

48. Letter
50. Comes close
53. Playground features
54. Foot levers
56. Flap
58. Food staple
59. Orderly
60. First name of Perry Mason's
    creator
61. Fragment
63. Type of soil
65. Expectorated
67. Cardinal's color
68. Poetic contraction
69. Compass point
71. Sextus' six
73. Continent (abbr.)

Crossword Puzzle No. 2

1. Come to terms
6. Egyptian deity
10. Cry of sorrow
14. Title of nobility
15. Overdue
16. Stringed instrument
17. Actor Markham
18. Riproarer (British slang)
19. Golfer's metal
20. Salamander
21. Sports official
24. Urban transport systems
25. Insect
26. Vex
28. Arbitrary
31. Undersized
33. Minimum
34. Deceived
35. Stallion's heartthrob
39. Ciphers (abbr.)
40. Pined
43. Daft

44. Poker stake
46. Edgar Lee Masters, e.g.
47. Another poker stake
49. Ecstasy
51. Word with vegetable or victory
52. Cree and Creek
55. Men's wear long out of style
56. Paddle
57. Windstorm
60. Lawyer's org.
63. Egg-shaped
65. Alexander Hamilton's downfall
66. "____ in the field of human conflict..." (Churchill)
68. Head in France
69. Or ____!
70. Turn inside out
71. Winter toy
72. Prepares
73. Small pies

DOWN

1. Apex
2. Boner
3. Smallest offspring
4. Within (prefix)
5. Time without end
6. Airborne
7. Window part

8. Journey (Latin)
9. Suitor's song
10. Miss MacGraw
11. Enticed
12. Small island
13. Be aware of
22. Head feature

138

23. Serpentine fish
25. Fuel
27. Shade tree
28. Arm bone
29. Inert element
30. Refuse nourishment
31. Begets
32. Suffix for measure or ease
34. Asian nation
36. Caught up in
37. Demolish (variant)
38. Surname of Sir Anthony
41. Chapters
42. Colorful scaleless fish
45. Diminish

48. Altar (Latin)
50. Permit
51. ____ willing
52. The late Mr. Shor
53. Composer of *Bolero*
54. Incensed
55. Stories
58. Pass judgment
59. Hornet's home
60. Declare
61. Mr. Lance
62. Crafts
64. Guided
67. Miss Gabor

Crossword Puzzle No. 3

1. Make a speech
6. 3.887 grams
10. Otherwise
14. Sudden fear
15. Glow
16. Fermented honey
17. Attempts
18. Small opening
20. Exist
21. Salt (Fr.)
22. Adolescent
24. Unsaturated hydrocarbon
26. Young woman
27. Culture medium
28. Coarse-grained rock
31. In an excited fashion
35. Too curious
36. Pat or Daniel
37. Regret
38. Sculpture, music, etc.
39. Naturally well-lit

40. Prefix for chute or medic
41. River (Sp.)
42. Land units
43. Arbor
44. Cutter of precious stones
46. Establishes
47. Alone
48. *Charley's* ____
49. Ballroom dance (var.)
52. Encircle
53. Onager
56. Loan to Marc Antony
57. Jugs
59. Eagle's home
61. Sea plant
63. Seed coat
64. Coat with sugar
65. Frost or Virgil
66. Door
67. Glowing coal

DOWN

1. Chooses
2. Uncommon
3. Indigo plant
4. Bind
5. Rapture
6. Borge and Anderson
7. Spoil
8. Curve
9. Expensive wood

10. Printer's measure
11. Tree part
12. Indian garment
13. Well-known garden
19. Make joyous
23. Letter
25. Before
26. "Here ____ ..."
27. Time periods

28. Growl
29. Waterwheel
30. Legal order
31. Hive yield
32. Pulled
33. Baited
34. *The Impossible* ___
36. Donkey
39. Reconstruction Republican
40. Fume
42. Southwestern brick
43. Thrall
45. Doctrine

46. Sable or mink
48. Two on the ___
49. Collect
50. Angel's headgear
51. Exhort
52. Coarse sand
53. Saudi
54. Dimensions
55. Prophet
58. Baseball abbreviation
60. Shade tree
62. To

1	2	3	4	5	■	6	7	8	9	■	10	11	12	13
14					■	15				■	16			
17					■	18			19	■	20			
21			■	22	23			■	24		25			
■	■	26				■	27				■	■	■	■
28	29	30			■	31				■	32	33	34	
35				■	36				■	37				
38			■	39				■	40					
41			■	42			■	43						
44			45			■	46							
■	■	47			■	48								
49	50	51			■	52				■	53	54	55	
56			■	57	58			■	59	60				
61			62	■	63				■	64				
65				■	66				■	67				

141

Crossword Puzzle No. 4

ACROSS

1. Tin or aluminum
5. Musical keys
10. Vasco da _____
14. Female voice
15. Wall decoration
16. Egyptian, for example
17. Leaks
19. Number associated with feline lives
20. Pharaoh's flow
21. The piper's son
22. Advocate
24. Partner of Marx
26. Poker beginning
27. Prepared speech
28. Merciful
31. Profits
32. Greek letter
34. Kind of board
35. Arum family plant
36. Disfigure
37. Competent
38. Periodical
39. Femur, e.g.
40. Physician for Fido
41. Score
42. Wood feature
43. Monogram of Her Majesty
44. Table decoration
45. Hypnotic state
46. Cheshire cat's expressions
47. X-ray shielding
48. Ruined
50. Fruit skin
51. Burro
54. Country road
55. Middle Eastern nation
57. Irish nationalist
59. Currier's partner
60. Type of beer
62. Ireland
63. Saucy
64. Crave
65. Snare

DOWN

1. Speedy
2. Margarine
3. Article
4. Cut off
5. .3937 inch (abbr.)
6. Thrust oneself
7. New York waterway
8. Follower
9. Drowsily
10. Indian sacred river
11. Character in *The Tempest*
12. Shopping center
13. Boys named for Lincoln
18. Optimistic

142

23. Highway (abbr.)
25. One of Columbus' ships
26. Swiss river
27. First name, heroine in *Cabaret*
28. Pant
29. Moderate brown
30. Thaw
31. Cheerily
32. Terror
33. Miss Dunne
35. Summons
36. Whimper
38. Delicately
39. Fastener

41. What lilies don't do
42. Class
44. Least moist
45. X
46. Someone given up for dead
47. Interior coating
48. Error
49. Cover the surface
50. Indian music
51. Moslem prince
52. Antitoxins
53. "One small ____ for man..."
56. Girl's name
58. N.Y.C. opera house
61. Radon (chemical symbol)

Crossword Puzzle No. 5

ACROSS

1. Bracelet adjunct
6. Tiny morsel
11. Novel by H. Rider Haggard
14. Biblical prophet
15. Vietnamese capital
16. Container for tea
17. "___ with Me" (hymn)
18. Friend (French)
19. Novelist's language
21. Extinct bird
22. Have sent
24. ___ Spirit (Noel Coward play)
25. Addendum (abbr.)
26. Celebrity
27. McDonald, e.g.
28. Flat-bottomed boat
29. Appreciative
33. City in Illinois, Georgia or Egypt
35. Polish
36. Singleton
37. Before (Latin)
38. Horse
39. Shekel
40. Drunkard
41. Headwear
42. Stops
43. Indefinite location
45. Mr. Hart
46. Undersized one
47. Red vegetable
48. New England state (abbr.)
50. Ebb
53. Ward off
54. Ewe's mate
55. Invert
56. Caspian, e.g.
57. Harangue
59. Cacophony
60. Penetrate
62. Irrigate
63. External (prefix)
64. Film spools
65. Indigent

DOWN

1. Chew noisily
2. Tramps
3. Location of 15 across
4. Crimson
5. Conductor
6. Conduct a meeting
7. Sloping driveway
8. Prefix for corn and form
9. Show Me state (abbr.)
10. Obsolete aircraft
11. Person from Edinburgh
12. Quiet

144

13. Thin sword
20. Hockey arena
23. Baled product
24. Undistinguished
26. Irritated
27. Big Boss
28. Simple song
29. And then _____ were none
30. Simpletons
31. Connected whole
32. Microscope part
33. House (Spanish)
34. Presently
35. Outset
38. Setting
39. Mold

41. Tremble
42. Square dance
44. Songbird
45. Males
47. Carries
48. Paired
49. Corundum
50. Impolite
51. Saga
52. One hundred to a dollar
53. Sense
54. Price
56. Therese, e.g. (abbr.)
58. Girl's name
61. Symbol for element found in electric signs

145

Crossword Puzzle No. 6

1. Salad type
5. Brutus' business suit
9. Relative pronoun
12. Nimbus
13. Evident
15. Exhibition
16. Handy timepiece
18. Roofing
19. Dead or Red
20. Successes
21. Laughed loudly
23. Part of Maine's nickname
24. Miss Bailey
25. Leapt
28. Frost
29. Pronoun
32. Office menial
33. Blends
34. Hair style
35. Odorous
36. Cures

37. Tight spot
38. Terminate
39. Aids to detectives
40. Mockery
41. Tiny
42. Confederate
43. Male goose
44. Moves rapidly
46. Dodge
47. Inform
49. Tender
50. Pointed implement
53. 50 across, for example
54. Regional features
57. Burden
58. Expression of contempt
59. Wanton look
60. Two make a quart (abbr.)
61. Gaelic
62. Thought

DOWN

1. Cutters
2. Trap
3. Melody
4. Used to be
5. Pulling
6. Egg-shaped
7. Becomes
8. Rainbow
9. "Eggbeater"

10. Pit
11. Due
14. Prepares a projector
15. Child's reward
17. Meditate
22. Boater's implements
23. Hyde or Central
24. Surveys
25. Nail relative

26. Flat surface.
27. Tryst
28. Intoxicating
30. Weight
31. Prefix for wear or tow
33. Corn and bone
36. Military headgear
37. Levee
39. Asian nation
40. Stunning defeat
43. Drain noise

45. Olive and linseed
46. Rock group led by the late Jim Morrison
47. Above
48. Injunction word
49. Mast
50. Mimicked
51. Cry of pleasure
52. Harp constellation
55. ____ of a kind
56. Miss MacGraw

Crossword Puzzle No. 7

ACROSS

1. Actor Heflin
4. Celerity
9. Brag
14. Past
15. Greeting
16. Detach
17. Make lace
18. Squid's defense
19. Polite
21. Prefix for hearse or verse
22. Intimation
24. Went down
25. Enclosure
26. Steeple
28. Fondles
29. Simple
30. Seed container, sometimes
31. Salutation
33. Contrive
34. Set down
35. Part of speech
38. White ____ snow
39. Solid
40. Merely
41. Mr. Jolson
42. Denuded
44. Clock part
45. Neckwear
46. Create
48. Lip
49. Talon
51. Loch _____ Monster
52. Locations
53. Mortar tray
54. Tempo
55. Hire actors
56. "_____ there a doctor..."
57. Neighboring planet
58. Liquid measure (abbr.)
59. Cut
62. Imperial
64. Milieu for Sutherland or Amara
66. Ram's mate
67. Trick
68. Designated
69. Drops of moisture

DOWN

1. Large container
2. Turkish title
3. Zilch
4. Glisten
5. Confined
6. B.P.O.E. member
7. Spanish article
8. Contribute
9. Dollar (slang)
10. "It takes ____ to know..."
11. Astatine (chemical symbol)
12. Begets pups

13. Wee
20. Example
23. Rage
24. Origin
25. Book part
26. Junk
27. Composure
28. Proper
29. Jealousy
31. Planter
32. At rest
34. Mortgage
36. Lift
37. Bestow happiness
39. Raced
40. Horse fodder

43. Good heavens!
44. Quick
45. Ratted
47. Motivation
48. Family member (slang)
49. Bird call
50. Luckless soul
52. Greens
54. Be obstinate
55. Worry
57. Provide workers
58. Jewel
60. Be obliged
61. Church part
63. Southern state (abbr.)
65. Atlantic state (abbr.)

Crossword Puzzle No. 8

ACROSS

1. Family
5. Piece
10. Intend
14. Carnival attraction
15. Toss
16. Binding
17. Saudi
18. Consumed
19. Miss Lanchester
20. Obstacles
22. Egg dish
24. Circus presentations
25. Building remains
26. Vexes
29. Engagement announcement
30. Infinitive word
32. Rates
33. Fine fellow
34. Arrange
35. Bewildered
36. Do away with

37. Babble
38. Morning moisture
39. Dodge
40. Not so common
41. Mr. Koch
42. Arduous journeys
43. Type of sword
44. Paris waterway
45. Be so bold
46. Second
48. Non-soldier
52. Deplaned
53. Employment
55. Theatre part
56. Location
57. Spring month
58. Rams' partners
59. Gardener, sometimes
60. Perseveres
61. Moms' mates

DOWN

1. Shellfish
2. Italian currency
3. Jewish month
4. The Cornhusker State
5. Linens
6. Learns
7. Rodents
8. Mother of Cain

9. Condemn
10. Shows off
11. Lazes
12. Church part
13. Tidy
21. Desserts
23. Fur animal
25. Elevate

26. Exchange
27. Comforted
28. Over
29. Fasteners
30. Uptight
31. Four-legged fisherman
33. Stopper
34. Clean prefix
36. Ultimate
37. Driven back
39. Ireland
40. Indian garment

42. Sway
43. Comes unwoven
44. Strike
45. Hand part
46. 1970 film set during Korean conflict
47. Mixture
48. Cutlass *et al.*
49. The Hawkeye state
50. Antique
51. Noted loch
54. Resort

Crossword Puzzle No. 9

ACROSS

1. Rodents
5. Throws
10. Golf score (two words)
14. Article
15. Willowy
16. Large amount (variant spelling)
17. Control
19. Sheer; uncontaminated
20. Hire
21. Lavish; profligate
23. Burden; duty
24. One who is attired
25. Wheedle
27. Pert girl
28. Mongol
32. Not in
33. Not warm
34. Computer product. Behold! (two words)

35. Gas or electric
37. Pals
38. Stoop
39. True
40. Golf ball holder
41. Dye
42. Believe
43. Dray
44. Floating
46. Leg (slang)
47. Value
50. Neckwear
53. Hindu garment
54. Burlesque
56. Malay sailing boat
57. Build
58. A simple whole
59. Sutured
60. Pintail ducks
61. Cloister

DOWN

1. Travel
2. Whit
3. Allure
4. Vine
5. American statesman
6. Inland islet
7. Salary
8. Chest
9. Sir: Sp.

10. Pronounced with breath
11. Stopple
12. Atmosphere
13. Spool; lively dance
18. Goddess of night
22. Small part
24. Shrewd; crafty
25. Sofa
26. Exaggerated

152

27. Nocturnal insect
29. Equal
30. Tree
31. A red pigment
33. Locust
34. Weight
36. Moon investigator
37. Pedal extremities
39. Arbitrate
42. Render harmless
43. Spiny plant

45. Reduces a vegetable to string-like consistency
46. Scout organization (abbr.)
47. Snakes
48. Peel
49. Front of ship
50. Performs
51. The second part of a minuet
52. Bristle
55. Frozen water

Crossword Puzzle No. 10

ACROSS

1. Hew
5. Mexican fiber plant
10. A court, as of a college (slang)
14. Italian currency
15. Angry
16. Impel
17. Affirm
18. Part of the skeleton
19. Plant of the bean family
20. Young animal
22. Something antiquated
23. Small table mat
24. Outer garment
25. Printer's measure
27. Beverage
28. Wedlock
32. Shake
34. Scoff
36. Sane
37. Biblical country
39. Turk

41. Hawaiian goose
42. Light boat
44. Surgical thread
46. Muscular twitching
47. Convey
49. Nevertheless
51. Pronoun
52. Stallion
53. Ship's crane
55. One who glides over the ice
58. Erasure
61. Steamship
62. French novelist
63. Burden
64. Wide-mouthed pitcher
65. Levels with the ground
66. Cupid
67. Clever people
68. Put forth, as force
69. Pointed weapon

DOWN

1. Common plastic earth
2. Bee structure
3. Mountain nymph
4. Talking bird
5. Hissing
6. Sarcasm
7. Chanted
8. Devoured

9. French article
10. Interrogation
11. Vases
12. Hindu god of fire
13. To distribute cards
19. Floats aloft
21. Falsehoods
22. In behalf of

24. Jewelry weight
25. Dispossess
26. Pertaining to the cheek
28. Measure
29. Assist
30. Plural of genius
31. Construct
33. Frog
35. Made comfortable
38. Fabulous animals
40. Supporter of a monarchy
43. Compound ether
45. Field of granular snow

48. Pelt
50. Named
53. Restrain from action
54. Coronet
55. Killed
56. Apteryx
57. Bane of tennis players (two words)
58. Nap
59. Scent
60. Bird habitation
62. Negligent
65. Concerning

Crossword Puzzle No. 11

ACROSS

1. National pastime
9. Period of the year
15. Zoological kingdom
16. Robe
17. Two-pronged instrument
18. Sizes up
20. Wink
21. European blackbird
22. Devour
23. Swedish singer
24. Last
25. Form of Charles
26. Wood of an E. Indian tree
27. Gasps
28. Fibrous Asiatic plant
29. Concerning
30. Centers
31. Defender of Troy
32. Attempts
33. Weight-raising device
34. Canary-like finches
36. Restrain
37. Thus
39. Inclining
40. Iron, e.g.
41. Morass
42. Swelling
43. Factions
44. Clare Boothe _____
45. Employ
46. Pitchers
47. Drum major's stick
48. Spruce up
50. Heavenly
51. Equalizer
52. Gems
54. Peruse again
55. Lacking plant ovules

DOWN

1. Idle talker
2. Distillate of indigo
3. Auxiliary railroad track
4. Edit
5. Financial institution
6. High in the musical scale
7. Chinese weight
8. Bemoans
9. Little
10. Facility
11. Babylonian god of the sky
12. Ribbon-like flag
13. Genus of Australian shrubs
14. Cuddles up
19. Epochs
21. Coal repositories
24. Passengers

25. Chair mender
27. Aim
28. Carousal
30. Brittle
31. Philippine Negritos
32. Verse of three measures
33. Europeans
34. Greeter
35. Not easily graspable
36. Edicts
37. Fleeting periods

38. Unity
40. Encounter
41. Vain
43. Turf
44. Former French statesman
46. Genus of tropical herbs
47. Feathered animal
49. Suffix meaning like
50. Letter
53. Pronoun

1	2	3	4	5	6	7	8		9	10	11	12	13	14
15								■	16					
17						■	18	19						
20					■	21					■	22		
23				■	24				■	25				
26			■	27				■	28					
29		■	30				■	31						
■	32					■	33					■		
34	35				■	36					■	37	38	
39				■	40				■	41				
42			■	43				■	44					
45		■	46				■	47						
48		49				■	50							
51				■	52	53								
54					■	55								

157

Crossword Puzzle No. 12

ACROSS

1. Store
5. Inexpensive
10. Loud sound
14. Pulled apart
15. Door part
16. Brink
17. Sharif or Khayyam
18. Appended
19. Latin for *marketplaces*
20. Well-being
22. Lifelike
24. Ailing
25. African mountains
26. Promontories
30. Fumed
34. Confederate
35. Theodore
36. Nab
37. Rodent
38. Defender of his country
40. Before (poetic)
41. Part of a flower
43. It's only human to
44. Festive
45. Wading bird
46. Alias
48. Dog genus
50. Hurok, e.g.
51. Neck feathers
54. Amanuenses
58. Competent
59. Loose Roman garment
61. Voice
62. Rend
63. Himalayan area
64. Food fish
65. Whirlpool
66. Playground apparatus
67. Agglomeration

DOWN

1. Store away
2. Where the heart is
3. Kind of examination
4. Faithlessness
5. Quack
6. Skin
7. Aim
8. Spies
9. Bicycle part
10. Denial
11. Scent
12. Site of the Taj Mahal
13. True
21. Entirety
23. Fortune telling card deck
25. Speak to
26. Irritating
27. Make happy

28. Part of church
29. Mesh
31. Gather by degrees
32. Kind of bird
33. Fantasy
36. To give out sparkles of light
38. Concerning punishment
39. Anger
42. Scornful imitation
44. Philistine giant

46. Part of flower
47. Coq _____
49. Snug retreats
51. Abominate
52. Lying down
53. Dressed
54. Winter vehicle
55. Sad
56. Famous volcano
57. Cleanser
60. Japanese sash

105

159

Frippery

ACROSS

1. Amulets
7. Contribute (two words)
13. Optimistic
15. Zealous pursuit of a cause
16. Narcotics
17. Replates
18. Well-being
19. Book of maps
21. Chair or bench
22. Rock or sand bars
23. Fish
27. Enraged
28. Head coverings
32. Parts of flowers
34. Strength
36. More subdued

37. Straighten
38. Iridescent
41. Spotted
43. Destructive insect or person
44. Penetrate
46. Indian weights
47. Popular martini ingredient
48. Pursuer of Moby Dick
52. Rabbit fur
53. The father of us all
57. Hereditary
59. Staining; pollution
61. Flow
62. Properties
63. Splatter
64. Chariot

DOWN

1. Black bird
2. Expectant desire
3. Continent
4. Actual
5. Get tangled
6. Solid part of fat
7. Iron vessel
8. Hovel
9. Egyptian goddess
10. Lose color
11. Thought
12. Place of retreat

14. Compound ethers
15. Skills
20. Meadow
23. Prohibit legally
24. Public warehouse
25. Tibetan priests
26. Small fish
28. Abets
29. Old-womanish
30. Ferocious animal
31. Smoothes by grinding
33. Silkworm

35. Befall
39. Stone implement
40. Intertwine
41. Invent
42. Sandy
45. Apex
48. Eras
49. Fiber from a plant
50. Stage of psychosexual development

51. Benevolent Enterprise, North America (abbr.)
53. Expression of pity
54. Note time of
55. Well advanced
56. Tableland
58. British goodbyes
60. Possessive pronoun

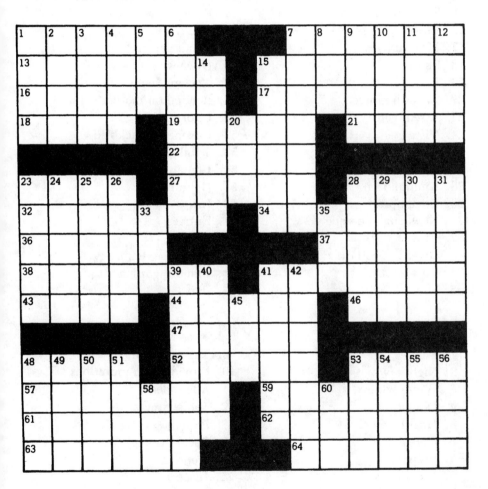

Underworld

25. Beat a schoolboy
27. Compete
29. Without effort
30. Boils
33. Flat plate
36. Part of a theater
37. Butter-making plant
38. Sword handle
39. Part of a church
40. Frigid
41. Obscure

43. Scanty
44. Drawing room
45. Imagine
46. Frock
47. Accustomed
49. Edible seed
52. Gentle
55. Private retreat
56. Japanese coin
58. Literary miscellany
59. Captained

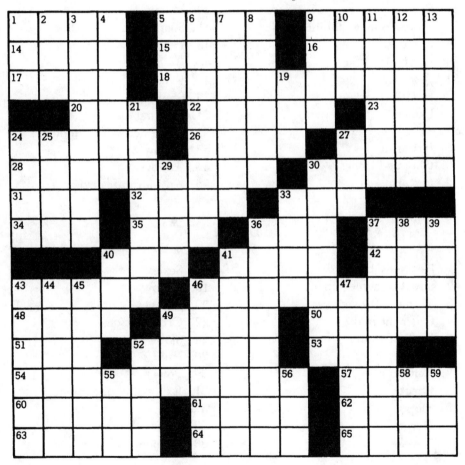

Odds and Ends

ACROSS

1. At ease
7. Inert
11. Meditated
12. Angrily
13. Happen
14. Ergo
15. Professional rehabilitator
16. Fame
18. Undivulged facts
21. Disorder
23. Health resort
25. Dunce
27. Skin
28. Irritating
30. Chopped fine
32. Perform

33. Joint
34. To exact punishment
35. Hunting dogs
36. Mischief makers
37. Finish
39. Marry
41. Soap froth
43. Learned
45. Barons
48. Eventful
49. Shuffling
51. Internal
52. Equipped with a motor
53. Throw
54. Annoys
55. Anti-aircraft device

DOWN

1. Heavenly body
2. Greatest achievement
3. Things left over
4. Garment maker
5. Rush of flame
6. Voter
7. Remittances
8. Czech
9. Slope
10. Heron
16. Revokes

17. Sexless
19. Follow
20. Japanese guitar
22. Cruel persons
24. Skill
26. Fruit seed
29. Power
31. Expressing discontent
32. Era
33. Cut with blows
38. Wanderers

40. Suspicious
42. Method of catching fish or criminals
44. Floods
46. Scanty

47. Like Shakespeare
48. Ascend
49. Purgative plant
50. Leg-of-mutton sleeve

Calling All Cars

ACROSS

1. What a tuned engine does
7. What an untuned engine does
13. What you can get for speeding
14. To work out (two words)
15. __/__ Flying Down to Rio
16. Preacher ____
18. Essential part of TV set
19. Opposite of motorist (abbr.)
20. Police racket squad
22. SE Asian New Year
23. Slice
24. Phone company dept. (abbr.)
26. Cylinders for small car engines.
29. St. or Henry
33. ____ Kleine Nachtmusick
34. ____ The Cows Come Home
35. Cry of Bacchus
36. What a flat tire can cause
38. The art of writing poems (arch.)
39. ____ José
40. ____ Lizzie.
41. Aid for a lost driver
44. Number of Snow White's Dwarfs
46. ____ ignition, dangerous engine condition
49. ____ Ben Adhem
51. Sadat's country
52. Composer Janacék
53. Accumulates a tab (two words)
55. Short electrical discharge
57. Guides the car
58. Pardon

DOWN

1. What good brakes help you do
2. A prison sentence
3. Battery ____ can corrode cables
4. Movie organization
5. Thee (Spanish)
6. Cocky walk
7. Unique
8. British thanks
9. Common inset
10. Uncouth person
11. Vital service for chassis protection
12. Printer's term
17. Not off
20. Big motor vehicle
21. Province in Canada (abbr.)
23. Indy '500' Pit ____
25. Important car air condition element
26. Washington's birth month (abbr.)
27. Change this at recommended times
28. Former United Nations initials

166

29. Car service area
30. ___ Been Working on the Railroad
31. Type of lettuce
32. Lock opener
34. Vital for saving gas, quick starts
37. Western Hemisphere Group
38. King ___, vital front end component
40. Concise
41. 4th planet from the sun

42. Border on
43. Southern corn bread
45. Neighbor of Md.
46. Home of the Incas
47. Troops loyal to General Park
48. Latin form of to be
50. Take regularly
52. Body of water in Quebec
54. Abraham's birthplace
56. Military shopping center

1	2	3	4	5	6		7	8	9	10	11	12
13							14					
15				■	16	17		■	18			
19			■	20			21	■	22			
■	■	23			■	24		25		■	■	■
26	27	28			■	29				30	31	32
33				■	34			■	35			
36				37			■	38				
■	■	39				40				■	■	■
41	42	43	■	44		45			■	46	47	48
49			50	■	51			■	52			
53				54		■	55	56				
57						■	58					

How to Solve Cryptograms

To some people a cryptogram is nothing more nor less than one of the milder forms of self-torture; but a lot of people think cryptograms are a lot of fun. If you thrill to tales of espionage and fantasize yourself a secret agent, you will find decoding cryptograms a fascinating pastime.

A cryptogram is a secret message in which one letter has been substituted throughout for another letter. To break the code, you have to figure out what each letter in the message really stands for.

This might seem altogether arbitrary and virtually impossible. But not so. Linguists have come up with a lot of information about the English language that is enormously helpful to cryptographers. They tell us, for example, that every English word includes one or more vowels, and that the five vowels—A, E, I, O, U— comprise 40 percent of all written communications. The letters L, N, R, S, and T comprise 30 percent of usage; and the letters J, K, Q, X, and Z comprise but 2 percent of usage. The remaining 11 letters comprise 28 percent of words commonly used in written English.

Armed with this information, you are ready to tackle any cryptogram. You might want to write each letter of the alphabet, followed by an equal sign, on a piece of paper. One-letter words, of course, are almost sure to be "I" or "A".

Examine the coded message to see how often each letter appears. It is a good hypothesis that the letter which appears most often stands for E. Examine especially the three-letter words. If the same three-letter combination appears frequently, and the third letter is also the letter that appears most frequently throughout, the chances are the word is THE. For example, if ABZ appears four or five times, and Z appears most frequently throughout, it is a fairly safe bet that ABZ stands for THE. Write T under A wherever it appears in the message; H under B; and E under Z.

Now examine the coded words again. If there are any two-letter words beginning with A (standing for T), the chances are the word is TO. Continue making educated guesses, changing your hypotheses whenever that becomes necessary, until you break the code.

Don't forget to time yourself. If you are a novice in cryptography, you're doing well to solve the cryptogram in Par score. As you become more proficient, aim for Medal score.

168

Historic Perspective

N Q K   E H M N   W M   H X R H U M
___   ____   __   _____

E W F N O J K M G O K   I W M N H B F K   X K B I M
_____   _____   _____

K B F Q H B N A K B N ,   L D J   W N   F D S K J M
_____ ,   ___   __   _____

N Q K   P J K H M U   M E D N M   D B   Q W M
___   _____   _____   __   ___

A H Z K M N U ' M   E X O A K I   Q H N   R W N Q   H
_____ _ _   _ _____   ___   ____   _

F Q H J W N H C X K   X H U K J   D L   I O M N
_____   _____   __   ____

A   B   C   D   E   F   G   H   I   J   K   L   M
‾   ‾   ‾   ‾   ‾   ‾   ‾   ‾   ‾   ‾   ‾   ‾   ‾

N   O   P   Q   R   S   T   U   V   W   X   Y   Z
‾   ‾   ‾   ‾   ‾   ‾   ‾   ‾   ‾   ‾   ‾   ‾   ‾

169

Boomerang

PAR SCORE: 32 minutes   MEDAL SCORE: 24 minutes

M W J   C J   A X M J   A M X Y H Q   S Y I
___ ___ _____ _____ ___

X A M J   A F J F   M B   V J Y F   M W J
_____ _____ __ ____ ___

E B A O X E M J F   M B   C J A X M J A E J
_____ __ _____

S W Y M   X I   M B B   K H J   G N J A M V Q
____ __ ___ _____

B O J   H V B B U J F   X I   M W Y M   C H X I   B A I
_____ __ _____ _____ ___

L J A J H Y M J   K Y H   Z B H J   Y A L J H
_____ ___ _____ _____

M W Y A   H J Z B H I J
____ _____

$\overline{A}$ $\overline{B}$ $\overline{C}$ $\overline{D}$ $\overline{E}$ $\overline{F}$ $\overline{G}$ $\overline{H}$ $\overline{I}$ $\overline{J}$ $\overline{K}$ $\overline{L}$ $\overline{M}$

$\overline{N}$ $\overline{O}$ $\overline{P}$ $\overline{Q}$ $\overline{R}$ $\overline{S}$ $\overline{T}$ $\overline{U}$ $\overline{V}$ $\overline{W}$ $\overline{X}$ $\overline{Y}$ $\overline{Z}$

170   (DIRECTIONS FOR SOLVING CRYPTOGRAMS ARE ON PAGE 168)

Mercy

PAR SCORE: 30 minutes   MEDAL SCORE: 15 minutes

```
AB   CDE   FGHI   JAO,   EKI   AO
__   ___   ____   ___    ___   __

XVIGKI   GLM   LDO   OD   FEZO.   CDE
_____   ___   ___   __   ____    ___

WGC   KFALI   VAUI   OFI   KEL   AL
___   _____   ____   ___   ___   __

OFI   OIWXIZGOI   NDLIK,   JAOFDEO
___   _____   _____    _____

KRDZRFALS.
_____
```

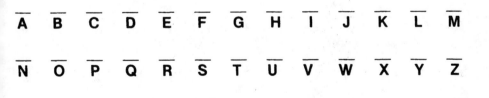

```
A  B  C  D  E  F  G  H  I  J  K  L  M
-  -  -  -  -  -  -  -  -  -  -  -  -

N  O  P  Q  R  S  T  U  V  W  X  Y  Z
-  -  -  -  -  -  -  -  -  -  -  -  -
```

(DIRECTIONS FOR SOLVING CRYPTOGRAMS ARE ON PAGE 168)   171

Ad by Artist

PAR SCORE: 46 minutes   MEDAL SCORE: 38 minutes

TZUEHJZ   TRBYYHUF
—————   ————————

HXTZAKUHBKE   TBCLCWHL
——————————   ————————

TWHULZC   EZZQE   EBRZXU
———————   —————   ——————

ETHUELZCHES   EKVIZALE   GBC
——————————   ————————   ———

JHEKWR   ELKYO.
——————   —————

A B C D E F G H I J K L M

N O P Q R S T U V W X Y Z

172   (DIRECTIONS FOR SOLVING CRYPTOGRAMS ARE ON PAGE 168)

Inanity

PAR SCORE: 90 minutes   MEDAL SCORE: 60 minutes

KGAUNA   MAWUGG   DONP   RCAJ
_ _ _ _ _ _   _ _ _ _ _ _   _ _ _ _   _ _ _ _

TIO   GUNP   WIJNOHAX   NOYYEWEAJP
_ _ _   _ _ _ _   _ _ _ _ _ _ _ _   _ _ _ _ _ _ _ _ _

FICGMUVE.   PCEN   HINP·   EHKIMPUJP
_ _ _ _ _ _ _ _   _ _ _ _   _ _ _ _   _ _ _ _ _ _ _ _

LOANPEIJ   AQEXAJWAN   CIR
_ _ _ _ _ _ _ _   _ _ _ _ _ _ _ _ _   _ _ _

WMTKPIZMUKCT   WUJ   XMEQA   IJA
_ _ _ _ _ _ _ _ _ _ _ _   _ _ _   _ _ _ _ _   _ _ _

HUX.
_ _ _

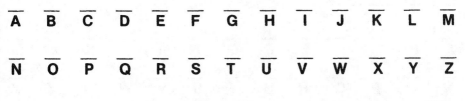

A̅   B̅   C̅   D̅   E̅   F̅   G̅   H̅   I̅   J̅   K̅   L̅   M̅

N̅   O̅   P̅   Q̅   R̅   S̅   T̅   U̅   V̅   W̅   X̅   Y̅   Z̅

(DIRECTIONS FOR SOLVING CRYPTOGRAMS ARE ON PAGE 168)   173

Down Under

PAR SCORE: 30 minutes   MEDAL SCORE: 18 minutes

YQT JYBTTYJ HU JFSVTF ETBT
___ _____ __ _____ ____

PMBTPSF UNMMTS ENYQ
_____ _____ ____

STYBNOPMNGTS VPYNZTJ, JHLT
_____ _____ ____

JYPBA VPATS. YQT CBHSNWNHXJ
_____ _____ ___ _____

OXRA EHXMS RBTPYT VH
____ _____ _____ __

NVYTBTJY NV YQT PXJYBPMNPV
_____ __ ___ _____

OHBV MPJJ. YQT VTEMF PBBNZTS
____ ____ ___ _____ _____

RHXMS OT NVJYPVYMF
_____ __ _____

SNJRTBVTS OF QTB LPNSTVMF
_____ __ ___ _____

OMXJQTJ.
_____

A	B	C	D	E	F	G	H	I	J	K	L	M

N	O	P	Q	R	S	T	U	V	W	X	Y	Z

    (DIRECTIONS FOR SOLVING CRYPTOGRAMS ARE ON PAGE 168)

Gourmet Note

PAR SCORE: 105 minutes
MEDAL SCORE: 75 minutes

BYPLG QKBGMR GQGL CVIX

_ _ _ _ _   _ _ _ _ _ _   _ _ _ _   _ _ _ _

BKSQKYMKH MKATYQR BKI UYQ

_ _ _ _ _ _ _ _   _ _ _ _ _ _ _   _ _ _   _ _ _

VYXYQR. MKLICKRI ZSGQNKJGX

_ _ _ _ _ _   _ _ _ _ _ _ _ _   _ _ _ _ _ _ _ _ _

QKBGMR BIXKRYX CVIX JYTQNISR

_ _ _ _ _ _ _   _ _ _ _ _ _ _ _   _ _ _ _   _ _ _ _ _ _ _ _

IBGMTGSI ZKATGXS BKGXPR.

_ _ _ _ _ _ _ _   _ _ _ _ _ _ _   _ _ _ _ _ _

Greatest Gift

PAR SCORE: 20 minutes
MEDAL SCORE: 8 minutes

J   MTOHRL   QJX   VHEE   KH
_   _____   ___   ____   __

THIPDRHL   UGH   QJBUHTSOHIH
_____   ___   _____

DM   RJUATH.
__   _____

No Rewards

PAR SCORE: 20 minutes
MEDAL SCORE: 8 minutes

STYMNSL   JEGJUY   D   FDYYQJ
_____   _____   _   _____

QTXY   GDS   FJ   MDQK   XT
____   ___   __   ____   __

RJQDSGMTQI   DX   D   FDYYQJ   ATS.
_____   __   _   _____   ___

(DIRECTIONS FOR SOLVING CRYPTOGRAMS ARE ON PAGE 168)

Kicks from a Bottle

PAR SCORE: 90 minutes
MEDAL SCORE: 60 minutes

L V D B Y K   T C J   D B Q   T M B   L V S   U D Z
_ _ _ _ _ _   _ _ _   _ _ _   _ _ _   _ _ _   _ _ _

V D G   O D K   B C L   G M S   V W A   B C J   V W K
_ _ _   _ _ _   _ _ _   _ _ _   _ _ _   _ _ _   _ _ _

U D Q   A D G   D F L.   K V Q   E M L   K Z Q ,
_ _ _   _ _ _   _ _ _   _ _ _   _ _ _   _ _ _

K V S   O C B   X C Q   N W D   U W B .
_ _ _   _ _ _   _ _ _   _ _ _   _ _ _

(DIRECTIONS FOR SOLVING CRYPTOGRAMS ARE ON PAGE 168)

Horns of a Dilemma

PAR SCORE: 25 minutes
MEDAL SCORE: 15 minutes

G A N J N   L F I N K   R   G B I N   B C   D B Q N,
_ _ _ _ _   _ _ _ _ _   _   _ _ _ _   _ _   _ _ _ _ ,

I E   P N R J   S D H S S N J,   O A N C   O N
_ _   _ _ _ _   _ _ _ _ _ _ _ ,   _ _ _ _   _ _

I H K G   G R V N   G A N   S H D D   S E   G A N
_ _ _ _   _ _ _ _   _ _ _   _ _ _ _   _ _   _ _ _

G R B D   R C P   Q R L N   G A N
_ _ _ _   _ _ _   _ _ _ _   _ _ _

K B G H R G B F C.
_ _ _ _ _ _ _ _ _ .

(DIRECTIONS FOR SOLVING CRYPTOGRAMS ARE ON PAGE 168)

Eternal Vigilance

PAR SCORE:	30 minutes
MEDAL SCORE:	15 minutes

H M P C   H M V H   K V A   R B D P   L G
‾ ‾ ‾ ‾   ‾ ‾ ‾ ‾   ‾ ‾ ‾   ‾ ‾ ‾ ‾   ‾ ‾

P O O P A H B V X   X B T P J H C   H F
‾ ‾ ‾ ‾ ‾ ‾ ‾ ‾ ‾   ‾ ‾ ‾ ‾ ‾ ‾ ‾   ‾ ‾

F T H V B A   V   X B H H X P   H P Z G F J V J C
‾ ‾ ‾ ‾ ‾ ‾   ‾   ‾ ‾ ‾ ‾ ‾ ‾   ‾ ‾ ‾ ‾ ‾ ‾ ‾ ‾ ‾

O V Q P H C   W P O P J D P   A P B H M P J
‾ ‾ ‾ ‾ ‾ ‾   ‾ ‾ ‾ ‾ ‾ ‾ ‾   ‾ ‾ ‾ ‾ ‾ ‾ ‾

X B T P J H C   A F J   O V Q P H C.
‾ ‾ ‾ ‾ ‾ ‾ ‾   ‾ ‾ ‾   ‾ ‾ ‾ ‾ ‾ ‾ ‾

Domestication

DP JDNJ DNJD YRCP NGB

‾‾ ‾‾‾‾ ‾‾‾‾ ‾‾‾‾ ‾‾‾

ODRFBIPG DNJD QRKPG

‾‾‾‾‾‾‾‾ ‾‾‾‾ ‾‾‾‾‾

DUWJNQPW JU CUIJXGP; CUI

‾‾‾‾‾‾‾‾ ‾‾ ‾‾‾‾‾‾‾ ‾‾‾

JDPZ NIP RTHPBRTPGJW JU

‾‾‾‾ ‾‾‾ ‾‾‾‾‾‾‾‾‾‾‾ ‾‾

QIPNJ PGJPIHIRWPW

‾‾‾‾‾ ‾‾‾‾‾‾‾‾‾‾

PRJDPI UC KRIJXP UI

‾‾‾‾‾‾ ‾‾ ‾‾‾‾‾‾ ‾‾

UC TRWODRPC.

‾‾ ‾‾‾‾‾‾‾‾

(DIRECTIONS FOR SOLVING CRYPTOGRAMS ARE ON PAGE 168)

Music to Your Ears

All of the 13 objects on the following pages are musical instruments. They derive from many countries. How many of them can you identify?

A score of 6 is good; 8 is excellent; and 11 is terrific.

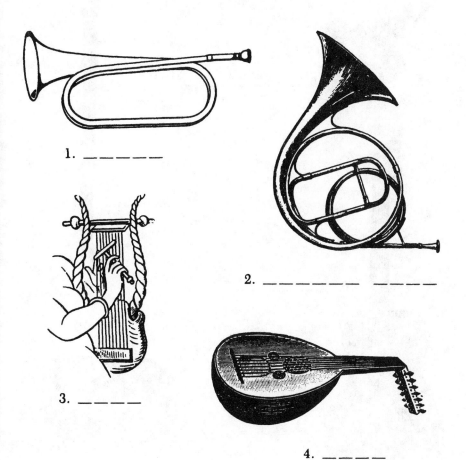

1. _ _ _ _ _

2. _ _ _ _ _ _ _   _ _ _ _ _

3. _ _ _ _ _

4. _ _ _ _ _

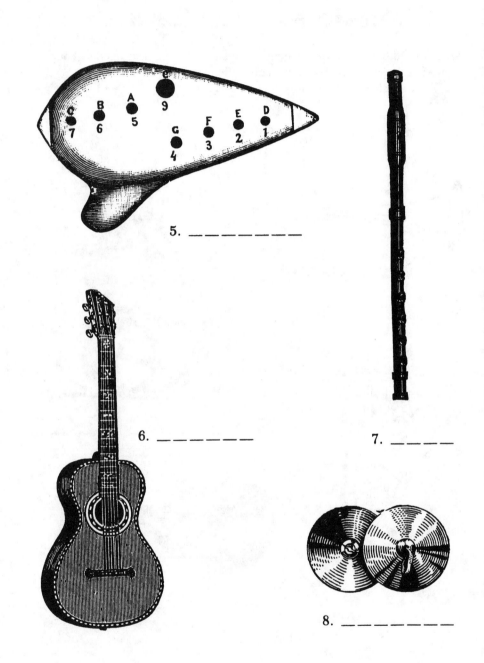

5. _ _ _ _ _ _ _ _

6. _ _ _ _ _ _ _

7. _ _ _ _ _

8. _ _ _ _ _ _ _ _

182

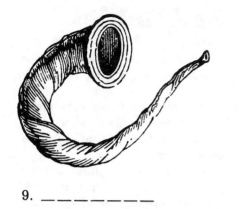

9. _ _ _ _ _ _ _

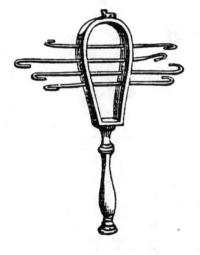

10. _ _ _ _ _ _ _

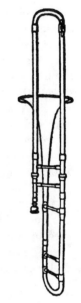

12. _ _ _ _ _ _ _ _ _

11. _ _ _ _ _ _ _

13. _ _ _ _ _ _ _

How to Solve Alfabits

The goal is to form as many words as you can out of the letters in the word which forms the given title. The answers are governed by the following rules:

1. Words must be at least four or five letters in length. The directions for each alfabit will specify. Plurals of two- or three- letter words (such as CATS or OXEN) are not allowed, nor are inflected forms of two- or three-letter verbs (such as GOES, EATS, BEEN or SEEING).

2. A word can be used in either the singular or the plural, but not both unless its plural changes the stem (e.g., MICE, GEESE, FEET, HOOVES). However, more significant additions are welcome: the use of ABLE does not preclude (provided the letters are available, of course) UNABLE, EN-ABLE, or ABILITY. Once a simple verb form is used, the addition of -(E)D, -(E)S or -ING is not allowed; LEARN is fine, but not also LEARNS, LEARNED, or LEARNING. If a verb's past tense changes the stem, however, all forms can be used (BEGIN, BEGAN, and BEGUN, for example). An adjective may be used in only one of its three degrees (DEAR, DEARER, or DEAREST).

3. Proper names and obsolete or archaic words are taboo. Reformed spellings (NITE for NIGHT, THRU for *through*) are forbidden.

Shepherd

There are at least 18 words of four letters or more in SHEPHERD. How many can you list? A score of 9 is good; 14 is a heap sight better.

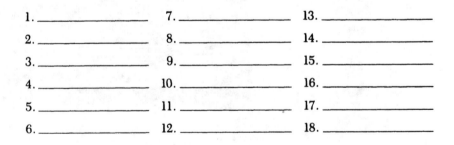

1. _____   7. _____   13. _____

2. _____   8. _____   14. _____

3. _____   9. _____   15. _____

4. _____   10. _____   16. _____

5. _____   11. _____   17. _____

6. _____   12. _____   18. _____

184

Anthracite

There are at least 37 words of five or more letters which can be made out of the letters of the word ANTHRACITE. How many can you find?

A score of 19 is good, 24 is above average, 30 is excellent, and 34 is worthy of sixteen rounds of applause.

1. _____

2. _____

3. _____

4. _____

5. _____

6. _____

7. _____

8. _____

9. _____

10 _____

11. _____

12. _____

13. _____

14. _____

15. _____

16. _____

17. _____

18. _____

19. _____

20. _____

21. _____

22. _____

23. _____

24. _____

25. _____

26. _____

27. _____

28. _____

29. _____

30. _____

31. _____

32. _____

33. _____

34. _____

35. _____

36. _____

37. _____

Chimera

There are at least 37 words of four letters or more that can be formed from CHIMERA. A score of 18 is good show; 25 is marvelous; and 33 is fantastic.

1. _____	13. _____	26. _____
2. _____	14. _____	27. _____
3. _____	15. _____	28. _____
4. _____	16. _____	29. _____
5. _____	17. _____	30. _____
6. _____	18. _____	31. _____
7. _____	19. _____	32. _____
8. _____	20. _____	33. _____
9. _____	21. _____	34. _____
10. _____	22. _____	35. _____
11. _____	23. _____	36. _____
12. _____	24. _____	37. _____
	25. _____	

Repulse

We found only 8 words of five letters or more in REPULSE. How many can you list?

A score of 4 or better is most attractive.

1. _____	4. _____	7. _____
2. _____	5. _____	8. _____
3. _____	6. _____	

Clairvoyant

At least 57 words of five letters or more can be formed from CLAIRVOYANT. A score of 28 is a vision; 38 is eye-opening; and 48 is out of sight!

1. _____
2. _____
3. _____
4. _____
5. _____
6. _____
7. _____
8. _____
9. _____
10. _____
11. _____
12. _____
13. _____
14. _____
15. _____
16. _____
17. _____
18. _____
19. _____
20. _____
21. _____
22. _____
23. _____
24. _____
25. _____
26. _____
27. _____
28. _____
29. _____
30. _____
31. _____
32. _____
33. _____
34. _____
35. _____
36. _____
37. _____
38. _____
39. _____
40. _____
41. _____
42. _____
43. _____
44. _____
45. _____
46. _____
47. _____
48. _____
49. _____
50. _____
51. _____
52. _____
53. _____
54. _____
55. _____
56. _____
57. _____

(DIRECTIONS FOR SOLVING ALFABITS ARE ON PAGE 184)

American

There are at least 36 words of four or more letters which can be made out of the letters of the word AMERICAN.

If you find 22, you're doing okay; 24 is obviously better; 26 is excellent; and 30 puts you at the very top of the class.

1. _____   13. _____   25. _____
2. _____   14. _____   26. _____
3. _____   15. _____   27. _____
4. _____   16. _____   28. _____
5. _____   17. _____   29. _____
6. _____   18. _____   30. _____
7. _____   19. _____   31. _____
8. _____   20. _____   32. _____
9. _____   21. _____   33. _____
10 _____   22. _____   34. _____
11. _____   23. _____   35. _____
12. _____   24. _____   36. _____

(DIRECTIONS FOR SOLVING ALFABITS ARE ON PAGE 184)

Recreational

There are at least 33 words of five or more letters which can be made out of the letters of the word RECREATIONAL. How many can you find?

A score of 16 is passing, 21 is above average, 25 is highly commendable, and 28 puts you way out front.

1. _____	12. _____	23. _____
2. _____	13. _____	24. _____
3. _____	14. _____	25. _____
4. _____	15. _____	26. _____
5. _____	16. _____	27. _____
6. _____	17. _____	28. _____
7. _____	18. _____	29. _____
8. _____	19. _____	30. _____
9. _____	20. _____	31. _____
10 _____	21. _____	32. _____
11. _____	22. _____	33. _____

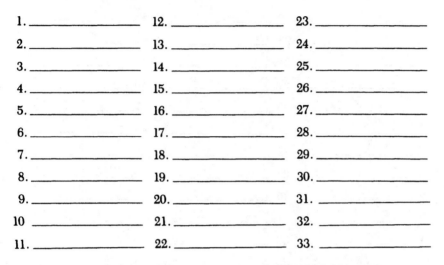

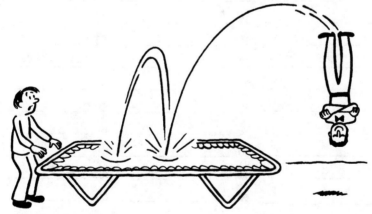

(DIRECTIONS FOR SOLVING ALFABITS ARE ON PAGE 184)

Buttermilk

At least 63 words of four or more letters may be found in BUTTERMILK. How many can you list?

A score of 30 is fine; 40 is rich; and 50 or more means you're the cat's meow.

1. _____	22. _____	43. _____
2. _____	23. _____	44. _____
3. _____	24. _____	45. _____
4. _____	25. _____	46. _____
5. _____	26. _____	47. _____
6. _____	27. _____	48. _____
7. _____	28. _____	49. _____
8. _____	29. _____	50. _____
9. _____	30. _____	51. _____
10. _____	31. _____	52. _____
11. _____	32. _____	53. _____
12. _____	33. _____	54. _____
13. _____	34. _____	55. _____
14. _____	35. _____	56. _____
15. _____	36. _____	57. _____
16. _____	37. _____	58. _____
17. _____	38. _____	59. _____
18. _____	39. _____	60. _____
19. _____	40. _____	61. _____
20. _____	41. _____	62. _____
21. _____	42. _____	63. _____

(DIRECTIONS FOR SOLVING ALFABITS ARE ON PAGE 184)

Distinct

We found just 7 words of four or more letters in DISTINCT. How many can you list?

A score of 4 or more is a distinct feat.

1. _____   3. _____   6. _____

2. _____   4. _____   7. _____

                              5. _____

Castanets

There are at least 30 words of four or more letters that can be formed from CASTANETS. Can you find them all?

A score of 15 shows you're clicking; 21 nets you applause; and 27 should be music to your ears.

1. _____   11. _____   21. _____

2. _____   12. _____   22. _____

3. _____   13. _____   23. _____

4. _____   14. _____   24. _____

5. _____   15. _____   25. _____

6. _____   16. _____   26. _____

7. _____   17. _____   27. _____

8. _____   18. _____   28. _____

9. _____   19. _____   29. _____

10. _____   20. _____   30. _____

(DIRECTIONS FOR SOLVING ALFABITS ARE ON PAGE 184)   **191**

Complexity

We listed 63 words of four letters or more that can be formed from COMPLEXITY. How many can you list?

Finding 30 is not simple; 42 shows an intricate mind; and 54 demonstrates profound verbal skill.

1. _____	22. _____	43. _____
2. _____	23. _____	44. _____
3. _____	24. _____	45. _____
4. _____	25. _____	46. _____
5. _____	26. _____	47. _____
6. _____	27. _____	48. _____
7. _____	28. _____	49. _____
8. _____	29. _____	50. _____
9. _____	30. _____	51. _____
10. _____	31. _____	52. _____
11. _____	32. _____	53. _____
12. _____	33. _____	54. _____
13. _____	34. _____	55. _____
14. _____	35. _____	56. _____
15. _____	36. _____	57. _____
16. _____	37. _____	58. _____
17. _____	38. _____	59. _____
18. _____	39. _____	60. _____
19. _____	40. _____	61. _____
20. _____	41. _____	62. _____
21. _____	42. _____	63. _____

(DIRECTIONS FOR SOLVING ALFABITS ARE ON PAGE 184)

How to Solve
Five-Letter Alfabits

The idea is to try to form as many words as you can out of the letters which compose the given title.

The answers are governed by the following rules:

1. Words should be composed of five-letter roots. Pluralizing four-letter words—such as HOURS, TARTS, MAKES, SENDS—is barred. However, if the spelling is completely changed in making the five-letter word, this is allowed.
2. Only one tense of a word may be used—either START or STARTED, TASTE or TASTES. However, different forms of a word may be used if they carry different meanings. For example, both RECEIVE and RECEIPT may be used, but not RECEIVED.
3. Foreign, obsolete, or archaic words are taboo. Reformed spellings are out.

Philodendron

There are at least 12 words, each of five letters or more, that can be made out of the letters in the word PHILODENDRON.

A score of 7 words is pretty good; 10 is outstanding.

1. _____	5. _____	9. _____
2. _____	6. _____	10. _____
3. _____	7. _____	11. _____
4. _____	8. _____	12. _____

Operational

There are at least 40 words, each of five letters or more, that can be made out of the letters in the word OPERATIONAL.

If you can find 22 of them, that's fine; 30 words is wonderful; and 35 is quite remarkable.

1. _____   14. _____   28. _____

2. _____   15. _____   29. _____

3. _____   16. _____   30. _____

4. _____   17. _____   31. _____

5. _____   18. _____   32. _____

6. _____   19. _____   33. _____

7. _____   20. _____   34. _____

8. _____   21. _____   35. _____

9. _____   22. _____   36. _____

10. _____   23. _____   37. _____

11. _____   24. _____   38. _____

12. _____   25. _____   39. _____

13. _____   26. _____   40. _____

27. _____

   (DIRECTIONS FOR SOLVING 5 LETTER ALFABITS ARE ON PAGE 193)

Discretionary

Out of the letters in the word DISCRETIONARY, one can theoretically make 41 words of five or more letters.

If you come up with 20, you are performing excellently. If you deliver 28, you're performing incredibly. And if you can fill in the spaces with 36 words, you can really puff up your chest.

1. _____   15. _____   28. _____
2. _____   16. _____   29. _____
3. _____   17. _____   30. _____
4. _____   18. _____   31. _____
5. _____   19. _____   32. _____
6. _____   20. _____   33. _____
7. _____   21. _____   34. _____
8. _____   22. _____   35. _____
9. _____   23. _____   36. _____
10. _____   24. _____   37. _____
11. _____   25. _____   38. _____
12. _____   26. _____   39. _____
13. _____   27. _____   40. _____
14. _____   41. _____

Consolidated

There are at least 17 words, each of five letters or more, that can be made out of the letters in the word CONSOLIDATED.

A score of 10 is very good; and 14 is terrific.

1. _____	7. _____	12. _____
2. _____	8. _____	13. _____
3. _____	9. _____	14. _____
4. _____	10. _____	15. _____
5. _____	11. _____	16. _____
6. _____		17. _____

Derisively

There are at least 16 words, each of five letters or more, that can be made out of the letters in the word DERISIVELY.

If you can fill in the spaces below with at least 10 words, that's very good; 12 words is first-rate; and 14 words gets you a blue ribbon.

1. _____	6. _____	12. _____
2. _____	7. _____	13. _____
3. _____	8. _____	14. _____
4. _____	9. _____	15. _____
5. _____	10. _____	16. _____
	11. _____	

(DIRECTIONS FOR SOLVING 5 LETTER ALFABITS ARE ON PAGE 193)

Conglomeration

There are at least 51 words, each of five letters or more, that can be made out of the letters in the word CONGLOMERATION.

If you can find 25 of them, you're doing fine; 35 is tremendous; and 45 words is absolutely outrageous!

1. _____   18. _____   35. _____
2. _____   19. _____   36. _____
3. _____   20. _____   37. _____
4. _____   21. _____   38. _____
5. _____   22. _____   39. _____
6. _____   23. _____   40. _____
7. _____   24. _____   41. _____
8. _____   25. _____   42. _____
9. _____   26. _____   43. _____
10. _____   27. _____   44. _____
11. _____   28. _____   45. _____
12. _____   29. _____   46. _____
13. _____   30. _____   47. _____
14. _____   31. _____   48. _____
15. _____   32. _____   49. _____
16. _____   33. _____   50. _____
17. _____   34. _____   51. _____

(DIRECTIONS FOR SOLVING 5 LETTER ALFABITS ARE ON PAGE 193)

Scholarship

There are at least 13 words, each of five letters or more, that can be made out of the letters in the word SCHOLARSHIP.

A score of 7 is dandy; 10 is just magnificent.

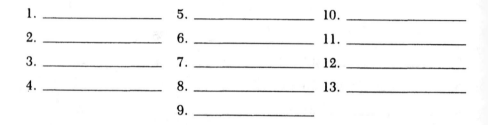

1. _____   5. _____   10. _____
2. _____   6. _____   11. _____
3. _____   7. _____   12. _____
4. _____   8. _____   13. _____
                      9. _____

Incantations

There are at least 22 words, each of five letters or more, that can be made out of the letters in the word INCANTATIONS.

If you can find 12 of them, you're pretty good; 15 is even better; and 18 puts you with the experts.

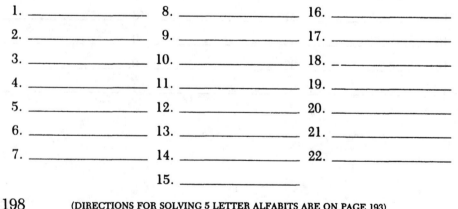

1. _____   8. _____   16. _____
2. _____   9. _____   17. _____
3. _____   10. _____   18. _____
4. _____   11. _____   19. _____
5. _____   12. _____   20. _____
6. _____   13. _____   21. _____
7. _____   14. _____   22. _____
                      15. _____

(DIRECTIONS FOR SOLVING 5 LETTER ALFABITS ARE ON PAGE 193)

How to Solve Blankies

The *Blankie* is based on progressive anagrams. Each Blankie is a short story in itself. In each story, a number of words have been omitted. Each omitted word is indicated by a number of dashes. Each dash represents a single letter. For example, a series of three dashes indicates a three-letter word; a series of four dashes, a four-letter word, etc.

The key word in the Blankie is set down in capital letters. Every successive word must include the letters contained in the previous word, plus one additional letter.

For example, with the key word AT, the successive words might be AT, CAT, TACK, STACK, TRACKS. Inferences drawn from the content should be of great help in suggesting the missing words.

At the Bank

S O you want to throw us a _ _ _. You'll waive one week's interest. Big deal!

You sit on that soft-cushioned swivel chair of yours and _ _ _ _ _ as a saint, and all the time you're taking us for two _ _ _ _ _ _.

You're so _ _ _ _ _ _ _, so at ease! You want us to make a _ _ _ _ _ _ _ of $100,000 in stocks as a guarantee for a $5,000 loan.

It's _ _ _ _ _ _ _ _ _!

A Bad Day

When he got to the beanery, John Michaelson sprawled down *A T* one of the rickety tables to __ __ __. After resting for a minute or so, he went over to the counter and got himself a portion of meat. He was famished and started to __ __ __ __ at his tough steak.

The __ __ __ __ __ here were low—about 75¢ for a sirloin that __ __ __ __ __ up at you as if to announce defiantly, "I'm as hard as leather, but what do you expect in a place like this?"

Everything about the joint was ill- __ __ __ __ __ __ __ __, but the worst of it was that he had left his wallet at home and wound up __ __ __ __ __ __ __ __.

Fowl Play

At the table *T O* which the waitress was sent, sat an old __ __ __. When she requested his order, he mumbled, "I like your __ __ __ __!' Flushing to her temples, she turned to go away, but he lurched forward and grabbed for her __ __ __ __ __, smirking, "Some chicken!"

She wheeled enraged, and slapped his face, snorting, "But not for an old __ __ __ __ __ __ __ * like you!"

* Add two letters.

(DIRECTIONS FOR SOLVING BLANKIES ARE ON PAGE 199)

The Difference Between Practiced Proficiency and Felicitous Facility

I A M of the opinion that innate ability is the absolute determinant of the "star" and that stage greatness is the fusion of genius and desire. Some directors, bloated with an egotistical confidence in their own ability to impart instruction, maintain that "every _ _ _ can be cured." I submit that the resultant products are then evaluated by comparative and therefore _ _ _ _ standards.

There is an unbridgeable _ _ _ _ _ which divides the talented and the taught. One _ _ _ _ _ _; the other labors; the one majestically treads the stage with a happy sureness; the other _ _ _ _ _ _ _ through a part with a painstaking and therefore painful precision.

(DIRECTIONS FOR SOLVING BLANKIES ARE ON PAGE 199)

The Puissance of Calm

In life, betimes, there arises A crisis which cannot be met simply with honest fortitude, but must be handled with consummate delicacy. _ _ such a time, what is required is not an _ _ _ which courageously throws down the gauntlet, but _ _ _ _ which convincingly evinces a comprehensive, _ _ _ _ _ appreciation of the situation. _ _ _ _ _ _ behavior, impressive by its very tranquility, may be, at such a juncture, more powerful _ _ _ _ _ _ _ _ than a dynamic ultimatum, justified from every standpoint but diplomacy.

202   (DIRECTIONS FOR SOLVING BLANKIES ARE ON PAGE 199)

Tightwad

The alarm went off. I heard a tap on the door.

"Excuse me, S I R, it's time for you to __ __ __ __ __."

From the street came the insistent shriek of a __ __ __ __ __ that kept on and on. I turned on my TV to get the news. What greeted my bleary eyes was the unwelcome sight of that miserable folk __ __ __ __ __ __ __, Jack Elephias Sower. I took a look at his puss, smirking, his arm __ __ __ __ __ __ __ on his guitar. Immediately, I turned off the set.

Some years ago, I had had a big scrap with that selfsame character about a restaurant bill. I'll never forget his nerve. A __ __ __ __ __ __ __ __ __ guy than Jack I've never met in my life. Although he had invited me and another friend to dinner, when the check came he recoiled as if it would bite him. And ever since I have been __ __ __ __ __ __ __ __ __ __ seeing him.

(DIRECTIONS FOR SOLVING BLANKIES ARE ON PAGE 199)

Sic Transit Gloria

There is a certain agency in London which makes a business of supplying noble escorts for American visitors at 25 pounds *P E R* __ __ __ __. By accepting such employment, a nobleman practically hangs a __ __ __ __ __ on his standing in society. From then on, he can consider himself socially defunct. And he knows it.

It is rather pitiful to see one of these big-time gigolos, abject, glory-shorn, with an insipid dowager on his arm, as he shamefacedly and coweringly __ __ __ __ __ __ through the portals of a mansion to attend a function which, had he retained wealth and position, he would have approached proudly and stalwartly, as one of the born elect.

But money is essential, and the touch of the royal __ __ __ __ __ __ __ which conferred a title did not confer a trust fund. What profit pomp and regality? What are needed now are __ __ __ __ __ __ __ __ __! Step right up, ladies, I'm tall, handsome, and a lord!

    (DIRECTIONS FOR SOLVING BLANKIES ARE ON PAGE 199)

A Helping Hand

Albright and wife arrived home from a vacation _T O_ find their house in shambles. _ _ _ of his mind with rage, Albright immediately sent for his caretaker, Crawford, whom he had hired just before he left.

Crawford arrived in the study to find Albright seated in his armchair. His feet, swollen with _ _ _ _, were propped up on an ottoman; his cheeks, swollen with fury, gleamed bright crimson.

"I _ _ _ _ _ to tear you limb from limb!" the old financier screamed at Crawford the moment the young man entered. "I go away for a week and look what happens! All I asked you to do was paint a few articles of furniture in the living room, and you've allowed the whole place to be destroyed!"

"I did finish the job, _ _ _ _ _ _ _," Crawford murmured sheepishly.

"You finished the job, all right!" Albright bellowed. "I've just been _ _ _ _ _ _ _ the room. You've painted _everything_, every piece of furniture, every wall, every last item in the confounded room, you bumbling fool!"

"Well," Crawford shrugged, "at least I'm _ _ _ _ _ _ _ _ _."

(DIRECTIONS FOR SOLVING BLANKIES ARE ON PAGE 199)

The Rewards Of Evil

AN angry girl was she as she __ __ __ after him. When she was __ __ __ __ enough to be in earshot, she shouted, "It was a trap and a __ __ __ __ __. There's no __ __ __ __ __ __ why you should have treated me this way. You promised me part of the take, but you gave it to me in phony bills. That's __ __ __ __ __ __ __."

Answers on page 127

Sore

Jane sat A T the table and __ __ __ __ her sandwich, impatiently waiting for her __ __ __ __ __. After she was __ __ __ __ __ __, she remained __ __ __ __ __ __, casting her eyes ever so often toward the entrance.

Finally, Tom entered and sauntered over to her. Jane was somewhat put out and met his greeting in silence.

Tom __ __ __ __ __ __ *, "You're as beautiful as ever, but right now, you look so darned __ __ __ __ __ __ *."

---

*Same number of letters as the previous word

(DIRECTIONS FOR SOLVING BLANKIES ARE ON PAGE 199)

Geriatrics

My *PA* likes to take a __ __ __ after dinner. It relaxes him after a stressful day.

He stretches out for a __ __ __ __ __ of an hour or so, and the __ __ __ __ __ in his limbs vanish.

If he wakes up suddenly before his hour is up, he __ __ __ __ __ __ __. He wonders where he is and he thinks his strength has left him. Then he jumps up, runs into the kitchen, and for a restorative, he consumes a full bowl of __ __ __ __ __ __ __.

Then, his energy fully restored, he sits down at the piano to play his favorite tunes, and you should hear that __ __ __ __ __ __ __ __.*

Two words

(DIRECTIONS FOR SOLVING BLANKIES ARE ON PAGE 199)

Just Desserts

It was AT the _ _ _ Baby, a restaurant of renown where the Black Bottom _ _ _ _ was the _ _ _ _ _ supreme.

We ordered just one portion and nominated Joan to be the first _ _ _ _ _ _. She took one spoonful and howled with delight. We knew the verdict.

So after Joan had served as the _ _ _ _ _ _ _ _, we each ordered one of those unimaginable delights.

Then we followed with two, three, and four apiece. None of us could stop—there were no _ _ _ _ _ _ _ _ _. Only the price of $2.50 each finally made us surrender. And, when we did stop, there wasn't a dry eye in the place. Everyone shed _ _ _ _ _ _ _ _ _* as we reluctantly departed.

*Two words

At the Shrink's

"My ego is blasted and my ID is in shambles. I just can't get _ _ _ of the _ _ _ _ fears that inhabit me.

"Tension _ _ _ _ _ through my every muscle and hatred and dread _ _ _ _ _ _ _ in my every pore.

"My _ _ _ _ _ _ _ are loathsome, and I am ashamed of the concepts that are _ _ _ _ _ _ _ _ _ _* of my befouled mind.

"Only thirty-nine people in all history had more cares and worries than I. Those men were all _ _ _ _ _ _ _ _ _ _ _."

*Add two letters to previous Blankie.

(DIRECTIONS FOR SOLVING BLANKIES ARE ON PAGE 199)

After the Homecoming

"You must have had a lousy time *AT* the beach. You sure came back with a good __ __ __, but your mood's been foul.

"You've been moving around as if you had __ __ __ __ __ in your __ __ __ __ __ __, and you __ __ __ __ __ __ __* me for just about anything. You've been as boorish as a __ __ __ __ __ __ __ __.

"Come on, Joe, be a little __ __ __ __ __ __ __ __ __. Is it possible that you're just plain hungry? Let's pile some grub on our __ __ __ __ __ __ __ __ __* relax in front of the TV."

Two words.

Fanaticism at the Bar

IN any cocktail party, the martini claims a sizable percentage of adherents, all of whom claim that __ __ __ should be severely dominant and vermouth low-keyed. I __ __ __ __ __ as I hear a martini afficionado __ __ __ __ __ __ out his special prescription to a group of drinkers __ __ __ __ __ __ around him. His proselytizing goes on with fanatic intensity.

"You drink my kind of martini or else you'll be socially damned," he implies. "Mine is the only proper __ __ __ __ __ __ __ __." To deny the only true faith is, according to such a zealot, __ __ __ __ __ __ __ __ __ the path toward alcoholic apostasy—it is, in fact, tantamount to __ __ __ __ __ __ __ __ __ __ from civilization itself.

(DIRECTIONS FOR SOLVING BLANKIES ARE ON PAGE 199)   209

Address Distressing

I'm AS _ _ _ _ as any woman can be who has to sit on a _ _ _ _ and listen to a lot of malarky from brainless femmes who just like to sound off. What a bore!

If I could spin the _ _ _ _ _ in my world, I'd arrange to spank every one of those fatuous, ego-ridden _ _ _ _ _ _ who, invited to address a group, come to the meeting unprepared, present no facts, and rattle on nevertheless, for half an hour or so, communicating nothing.

Such a pompous, vapid jackass _ _ _ _ _ _ _ any serious organization. You would think, with the choice of speakers they have, they would manage to find someone who could be just a little _ _ _ _ _ _ _ _* than this.

*Two words.

The Literati

There is, TO a certain extent, a hierarchy in the world of belles-lettres. To _ _ _ _ the writer who currently occupies the pinnacle _ _ _ _ in the field requires nothing less than extraordinary talent.

_ _ _ _ _ may be inspired, but their faces hardly ever grace a _ _ _ _ _ _. One can't win acclaim in literature through good looks.

Nor, in the literary field, is recognition obtained through a duel of wits. The best _ _ _ _ _ _ _ _ is a touch of genius. Neither _ _ _ _ _ _ _ _* guile will yield any response.

*Two words.

(DIRECTIONS FOR SOLVING BLANKIES ARE ON PAGE 199)

Spelling Bee

It seems that accuracy in spelling is rapidly becoming a lost art. However, if you're involved in the academic, literary, or even the business world, the kind of visual acuity and painstaking attention to detail that go into good spelling are highly valuable characteristics.

Listed below are 50 words which are commonly misspelled. If you think the word is spelled correctly, put a check in the column marked RIGHT. If you think the word is spelled incorrectly, put a check in the column marked WRONG. Then write in the correct spelling in the last column.

The scoring is tricky. If the word is spelled correctly and you have so marked it, you get one point. If you say the word has been spelled correctly and it is actually wrong, you lose one point. If the word is spelled incorrectly and you mark it as wrong, you score two points. If you then write out the proper spelling, you score an additional three points.

A score of 60 will get you through grammar school; 90 makes you college material; and 120 gets you into Phi Beta Kappa.

	RIGHT	WRONG	CORRECT SPELLING
1. Caterpillar			
2. Finagle			
3. Javalin			
4. Apparatus			
5. Traceable			
6. Seige			
7. Curriculam			
8. Roughage			
9. Abscess			
10. Myrhh			
11. Frankinsence			

	RIGHT	WRONG	CORRECT SPELLING
12. Inviegle	_____	_____	_____
13. Seize	_____	_____	_____
14. Weird	_____	_____	_____
15. Abhorrant	_____	_____	_____
16. Accoustics	_____	_____	_____
17. Acumin	_____	_____	_____
18. Adhesion	_____	_____	_____
19. Incorrigible	_____	_____	_____
20. Irredescent	_____	_____	_____
21. Negroes	_____	_____	_____
22. Innocuous	_____	_____	_____
23. Candelabrum	_____	_____	_____
24. Batallion	_____	_____	_____
25. Viscous	_____	_____	_____
26. Sacrilegious	_____	_____	_____
27. Bizarre	_____	_____	_____
28. Heliatrope	_____	_____	_____
29. Rigmarole	_____	_____	_____
30. Forcemeet	_____	_____	_____
31. Vinegary	_____	_____	_____
32. Combustible	_____	_____	_____
33. Finnese	_____	_____	_____
34. Garrolous	_____	_____	_____
35. Sarcophogus	_____	_____	_____
36. Silhouette	_____	_____	_____
37. Catastrophies	_____	_____	_____

212

	RIGHT	WRONG	CORRECT SPELLING
38. Embarrass	_____	_____	_____
39. Pharoah	_____	_____	_____
40. Cuneiform	_____	_____	_____
41. Celluloid	_____	_____	_____
42. Heinous	_____	_____	_____
43. Pommaid	_____	_____	_____
44. Panegyric	_____	_____	_____
45. Appendicitis	_____	_____	_____
46. Villify	_____	_____	_____
47. Raucous	_____	_____	_____
48. Bronchitus	_____	_____	_____
49. Doberman pincher	_____	_____	_____
50. Sassparilla	_____	_____	_____

How Creative are You?

Creativity demands imagination, the ability to improvise, and the courage to combine and utilize known facts in new ways.

We are repeatedly warned that we are wearing out the resources of the world, that we ignore or discard valuable material which could be put to excellent use. This intriguing quiz asks you to scratch your gray cells a bit to see if you can come up with some novel or unexpected answers or solutions to some common and some unusual questions.

In each of the following situations, select the response that would be nearest your own:

1. You have just bought a new typewriter that doesn't work properly. You would:
   a. Tinker with it in the hope of solving the problem.
   b. Pack it and return it to the place of purchase.
   c. Ask a friend or neighbor to help you.

2. The box which held the typewriter contained paper wrapping and Styrofoam packing. You would:
   a. Throw out the box as well as the other packing items.
   b. Come up with an immediate idea about how to use the packing material.
   c. Put the packing material away with the thought that it might come in handy later.

3. In your living quarters, you find a hole in the wall. You would:
   a. Get the needed materials and attempt to repair it yourself.
   b. Do nothing about it.
   c. Hire a repairman to fix it.

4. At some time or other during your life have you:
   a. Possibly written a poem as an assignment, but never voluntarily.
   b. Written one or more poems which you have voluntarily shared with others.
   c. Written some poems which you hid or threw away.

214

5. You have just tried a simple home-project, such as hanging a shelf, following a recipe, gardening. Your effort was unsuccessful. Would you:
    a. Feel discouraged and never try again.
    b. Discard what you did, but approach the same project another way.
    c. Use whatever you spoiled for something else, if possible.

6. You are a new employee in a business which has a set pattern of operation. You would:
    a. Follow the prescribed routine.
    b. Make your own adjustments provided they don't disturb others.
    c. Talk over your suggestions with your immediate superior.

7. You are gazing at the clouds. You:
    a. See forms in them.
    b. Try to predict the weather.
    c. See them only as clouds.

8. When watching a mystery TV show or movie, or reading a suspense book, do you prefer:
    a. To know "who-done-it" and observe how the sleuth solves it.
    b. To pick up clues along the way so you can try to figure it out yourself.
    c. To just relax and enjoy the plot without having to figure it out.

9. Do you think that most creative people are:
    a. Emotionally stable.
    b. Emotionally unstable.
    c. Average people with creative talents.

10. You are moving to a new city, town, or country where the life-style is rather different from the one you've been used to. Which would be most important to you:
    a. Following the pattern of the new community.
    b. Doing pretty much as you always have done.
    c. Integrating your old way of life into the new environment.

11. For recreation, do you usually prefer:
    a. Sports.
    b. Reading, TV, or movies.
    c. Creating things.

12. You suddenly find yourself on a deserted island in the South Pacific with only a good substantial knife. The island has birds, vegetation, and a waterfall. In such a situation do you think you:
    a. Would soon go mad.
    b. Would probably die in a relatively short time.
    c. Could sustain yourself for a long period.

13. You are with a group of people who are discussing unfamiliar scientific topics. Would you:
    a. Wish you weren't there.
    b. Ask questions so you could learn about the topic.
    c. Listen carefully to learn how the conversation applies to your life.

14. The telephone rings. You are invited to attend a masquerade party in a half hour. Would you:
    a. Refuse the invitation because you have nothing to wear.
    b. Find something in your closet to improvise a costume.
    c. Go wearing your normal clothing.

15. You have planned a picnic for your mate's birthday. You have invited several others to join you. That morning it starts to rain. Would you:
    a. Cancel the whole party.
    b. Quickly make new plans for everybody.
    c. Cancel the picnic and eat alone with your mate instead.

16. Your job has been phased out, leaving you out of work. Would you:
    a. Evaluate your talents and try a new field.
    b. Read the want ads and look for the same kind of job.
    c. Join the unemployment line.

17. Is it your belief that:
    a. There is no such thing as intuition.
    b. You possess a degree of intuition.
    c. Some of your friends are intuitive, but not you.

216

Answers

1. *Peter Pan*
2. Pantheon
3. Panorama
4. Rampant
5. Pantaloons
6. Sampan
7. Panacea
8. Pandemonium
9. Panhandle
10. Pantomime
11. Pancreas
12. Pancake
13. Pansy
14. *Gargantua and Pantagruel*
15. Pandora
16. Sancho Panza
17. Panache
18. Panda
19. Panegyric
20. Spaniel
21. Panzer
22. Companion
23. Company
24. Pancho Villa
25. Tympan
26. Hispanic
27. Campanile
28. Expand
29. Pant
30. Lepanto

1. Shortage
2. Belongings
3. "Short People"
4. Strawberry shortcake
5. "The long arm of the law"
6. Shorthanded
7. Henry Wadsworth Longfellow
8. Shortstop
9. Long John Silver
10. Short-lived
11. "It's a Long Way to Tipperary"
12. Short story
13. "Long Tall Sally"
14. Short-order cook
15. Longitude
16. Bermuda shorts
17. Crawford W. Long
18. Shortwave
19. *The Longest Day*
20. Shortcomings
21. Huey P. Long
22. Short-winded
23. Prolong
24. Make a long story short
25. "Tomorrow Belongs to Me"
26. Longobard
27. Short-circuit
28. Long Kesh
29. Shortening
30. Longshot
31. Jockey shorts
32. Longines
33. Short ribs
34. Long bow
35. Shorthand
36. "The Long and Winding Road"
37. *Short Eyes*
38. Longhair
39. Shortcut
40. *Long Day's Journey into Night*
41. Make short work (or shrift) of
42. Longshoreman
43. Shortsighted
44. Furlong
45. "Short'nin' Bread"
46. Daddy longlegs
47. Short end of the stick
48. Oolong
49. Short snort
50. Longevity
51. The long and the short and the tall
52. Klong
53. "My Heart Belongs to Daddy"
54. Short-term
55. In the long run

1. Irving Berlin
2. Virginia Dare
3. Texas Guinan
4. Stephen Birmingham
5. Jack London
6. India Wilkes
7. Nathan Detroit
8. Georgia O'Keeffe
9. Anatole France
10. Robert Indiana
11. Buffalo Bill
12. Virginia Woolf
13. Morey Amsterdam

1. Vanish
2. Pennsylvania
3. Vandal
4. Relevant
5. Cyrus Vance
6. Ivan the Terrible
7. Advantage
8. Dick Van Dyke
9. Martin Van Buren
10. Vancouver
11. Evanescent
12. Vanadium
13. Evangelists
14. Vivian Vance
15. Caravan
16. Vanilla
17. *Avanti*
18. Silvanus
19. *Vanity Fair*
20. Van Dyck or Van Dyke
21. Erevan or Yerevan
22. Contrivance
23. Vanguard
24. Vanderbilt
25. Dame Edith Evans
26. Vanquish
27. Sylvania
28. *Evangeline*
29. Transylvania
30. Vanessa Redgrave

WATCH IT! .... page 14

1. Batch
2. *Catcher in the Rye*
3. Latch
4. Satchel
5. *To Catch a Thief*
6. Hatch
7. Atchison, Topeka, and Santa Fe
8. Watchword or catchword
9. Hatchet
10. Natch
11. Sasquatch
12. Patch
13. Snatch
14. *Watch on the Rhine*
15. Ratchets
16. Thatched
17. Catcher
18. Natchez
19. Three on a match
20. "Watch the birdie"
21. Cowcatcher
22. "Catch a Falling Star"
23. Deathwatch
24. Dispatch
25. Catch as catch can
26. Scratch
27. "Matchbox"
28. Swatch
29. Saskatchewan
30. *Catch-22*
31. Cratchit
32. Nurse Ratched
33. *The Matchmaker*
34. *A Patch of Blue*

IT'S ABOUT TIME .... page 16

1. Ragtime
2. In no time at all
3. Timepiece
4. *Of Time and the River*
5. *Time on My Hands*
6. Time and tide wait for no man
7. To two-time
8. Time and again
9. *Summertime*
10. Greenwich Time
11. Timeclock
12. Timeless
13. Times Square
14. *The Time of Your Life*
15. Good-time Charley
16. Father Time
17. Time out of mind
18. Overtime
19. Behind the times
20. Once upon a time
21. To do time

SALLY FORTH .... page 17

1. Salmon
2. Nasal
3. Salem
4. Salt
5. Salad days
6. Rehearsal
7. Saliva
8. Dr. Jonas Salk
9. Sal Mineo
10. Salient
11. Saloon
12. Psalm
13. Salt Lake City
14. *Salambo*
15. Salamander
16. Missal
17. Taken with a grain of salt
18. Sally Bowles
19. Rosalind Russell
20. Salami
21. Salisbury
22. Salvo
23. Pablo Casals
24. Salad
25. Basalt
26. Salutation
27. Salmonella
28. *Death of a Salesman*
29. Thessaly
30. Vassal
31. El Salvador
32. Salt of the Earth
33. Absalom
34. Saluki
35. Dar es Salaam
36. Salome
37. Sally Rand
38. *Pharsalia*
39. Salver
40. Robert de la Salle
41. Saltimbocca
42. Antonia Salazar
43. Psaltery
44. Salvage
45. Salon
46. Sallow
47. Upsala
48. Salmagundi
49. Salutary, or salubrious
50. Saladin
51. Dorsal
52. Salvador Dali
53. J.D. Salinger
54. Marsala
55. Salzburg
56. Salvation Army
57. Felix Salten
58. Jerusalem
59. Salacious
60. Valeria Messalina

THE LOWDOWN .... page 20

1. Below
2. Yellow
3. Clown
4. Flowing
5. Allow
6. Pillow
7. Odd Fellow
8. Flower
9. Glower
10. Slowdown
11. Swallow
12. Henry Wadsworth Longfellow
13. Shallow
14. "Low man on the totem pole"
15. Fellow traveler
16. Weeping willow
17. Low Countries
18. Tallow
19. Plowshares
20. *Mayflower*
21. Mellow
22. Follow
23. Jean Harlow
24. "Flower children"
25. Slow-motion
26. Marshmallows
27. Bellows
28. *The Flowering Peach*
29. Hollow
30. Saul Bellow
31. Juliette Low
32. "Blowin' in the Wind"
33. *Pillow Talk*
34. Gallows
35. Christopher Marlowe
36. "Swing Low Sweet Chariot"
37. Lowbrow
38. Amy Lowell
39. Make allowances for
40. Malcolm Lowry

218

1. Stomach
2. Macaw
3. Douglas MacArthur
4. Macramé
5. Ted Mack
6. Machete
7. Macadam (or tarmac)
8. Immaculate
9. Macaroni
10. Sumac
11. *The Time Machine*
12. Macy's
13. Mackerel
14. Grimace
15. Smack
16. *Macbeth*
17. Antimacassar
18. *Danse Macabre*
19. *MacMillan and Wife*
20. James Ramsay MacDonald
21. *Merrimack*
22. Emaciated
23. Macron
24. Niccolo Machiavelli
25. Macedonia
26. Macadamia
27. Mack the Knife
28. Macao
29. Smacker
30. Maccabees
31. Hammacher Shlemmer
32. Macaroon
33. "Mother Machree"
34. Telemachus
35. Macintosh
36. *Andromache*
37. Archibald MacLeish
38. Macduff
39. *The Short and Happy Life of Francis Macomber*
40. The grand climacteric

1. Ding dong bell
2. Campbell's
3. Belligerent
4. Liberty Bell
5. Griffin Bell
6. Belle of the ball
7. Bellow
8. Edward Bellamy
9. Clarabelle
10. *For Whom the Bell Tolls*
11. Belladonna
12. Ante-bellum
13. Bellybuster or belly-flop
14. Bellini
15. Bellwether
16. Hubbell Gardner
17. Embellish
18. Bellicose
19. Ma Bell
20. *A Bell for Adano*
21. Belly dancer
22. Boxer Rebellion
23. Bella Abzug
24. Bellerophon
25. Saul Bellow
26. Belle Watling
27. Barbells or dumbbells
28. Bellybutton
29. *Bell, Book and Candle*
30. Hell's bells
31. Whiskey Rebellion
32. *Sunrise at Campobello*
33. Ralph Bellamy
34. *The Bells of St. Mary's*
35. James Branch Cabell
36. Vincenzo Bellini
37. *The Bell Jar*
38. Bell-bottoms
39. Maybelline
40. Bellboy or bellhop
41. Rubella
42. Ida M. Tarbell
43. *If I Were a Bell*
44. *Belle de Jour*
45. Belleek ware

1. Chimney
2. Therapy
3. Whim
4. Sheriff
5. Sashimi
6. Ether
7. Chimpanzee
8. Thermos
9. Chime
10. Sherwood Forest
11. "A Hymn to Him"
12. Gherkin
13. Thimble
14. *The Shoes of the Fisherman*
15. Himalayas
16. Cherish
17. Chimerical
18. Cherbourg
19. Archimedes
20. Weather
21. Whimper
22. Inherent
23. Hiroshima
24. Christopher (St.)
25. Shimmer
26. Sherman (William Tecumseh)
27. Mishima
28. Panther
29. Hercules
30. Cherub
31. Whimsy
32. Wither
33. Himmler (Heinrich)
34. Sheraton (Thomas)
35. Shimmy

1. The doctor
2. William Tell
3. John Chapman, better known as Johnny Appleseed
4. The Apple of Discord
5. Snow White
6. The teacher
7. Apple polisher
8. Adam's apple
9. The Bible; Psalms17:8 and Proverbs 7:2
10. Don't upset the apple cart
11. Apple jack (calvados)
12. Sir Edward Victor Appleton

1. Calories
2. Local
3. California
4. Political
5. Calliope
6. Cal Tech
7. Calm
8. Musical
9. Lauren Bacall
10. Decalcomania
11. Caligula
12. Scallion
13. Calf
14. Calvary
15. Escalator
16. Calcium
17. Calvin Coolidge

18. Umbilical cord
19. Critical
20. Calico (or percale)
21. Calendar
22. Calamitious
23. Recalcitrant
24. Scald
25. Caledonia
26. Logical
27. Scalawags
28. *The Little Rascals*
29. Tuscaloosa
30. Catcall
31. Supercalifra-
gilisticexpia-
lidocious
32. Scalp
33. Calumny

34. Mythical
35. Scalpel
36. Calisthenics
37. Mescaline
38. Calculus
39. John Calvin
40. Scallop
41. Calligraphy
42. Optical
43. Baccalaureate
44. Callous
45. Antithetical
46. Caliban
47. "Magical
Mystery Tour"
48. Recall
49. Topical
50. Calomine lotion

HOW IN THE WORLD? .... page 34

1. Howl
2. Shower
3. Julia Ward Howe
4. Chow
5. *The Last Picture Show*
6. The Show Me State
7. Howard Cosell
8. "How do I love thee?"
9. Ron Howard
10. "How now, brown cow?"
11. April Showers
12. Elias Howe
13. Chowder
14. "Show Me!"
15. *Dr. Strangelove or: How I Learned to Stop Worrying and Love the Bomb*
16. Dwight David Eisenhower
17. *The Late Show*
18. By a show of hands
19. *Your Show of Shows*
20. Howdah
21. *How the West Was Won*
22. William Howard Taft
23. Howland Owl
21. *How Now, Dow Jones?*
25. *The Greatest Show on Earth*
26. Howitzer
27. Howdy Doody
28. Leslie Howard
29. "There's No Business Like Show Business"
30. *How Green Was My Valley*
31. Showdown
32. Sidney Howard
33. Show and tell
34. William Dean Howells
35. Somehow or other

36. *How to Win Friends and Influence People*
37. Showpiece
38. *Showboat*
39. Chow mein
40. *Howard's End*

DAYDREAMING .... page 37

1. *Long Days Journey into Night*
2. "Tomorrow is another day."
3. "Rome wasn't built in a day."
4. Ash Wednesday
5. *Happy Days*
6. ". . . a day in June"
7. Dennis Day
8. Friday
9. *Anne of the Thousand Days*
10. D-Day
11. *Days of Wine and Roses*
12. *Daybreak*
13. "A Day in the Life"
14. *Day of the Locust*
15. Dog days
16. *Day of the Jackal*
17. Easter Monday
18. Day of Reckoning or Day of Judgement
19. Payday
20. *A Day in the Life of Ivan Denisovich*
21. *The Day the Earth Stood Still*
22. Washington's Birthday
23. *Seven Days in May*
24. Dayton
25. Moshe Dayan
26. "Monday, Monday"
27. *Dog, Day Afternoon*
28. Independence Day
29. Doris Day
30. Bastille Day
31. ". . . to a summer's day"
32. *Queen for a Day*
33. *Sunday, Bloody Sunday*
34. "Thirty days hath September. . ."
35. *On a Clear Day You Can See Forever*
36. *Happy Birthday, Wanda June*
37. *Never on Sunday*
38. Days of Rage
39. "Yesterday"
40. *Around the World in Eighty Days*
41. Thursday's child
42. Thank God It's Friday
43. Doubleday
44. Clarence Day
45. A year and a day
46. Michael Faraday
47. Every dog has his day
48. "My Day"
49. Day of Atonement
50. Call it a day

220

IN COLD BLOOD .... page 43

The answer to this perplexing problem is to be found in the fact that it is a tenet of the law in all civilized countries that the innocent may not be made to suffer with the guilty. The sisters were Siamese twins.

THE MUNICIPAL RAILWAYS ...... page 44

The illustration shows the required directions for the five lines, so that no line shall ever cross another.

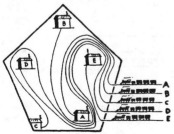

THE DEAD TOURIST .... page 45

Seeing Mrs. Elkins' picture in the Boston society column, and reading the details of the tragic death of her husband, Mr. Harper remembered that Mrs. Elkins had been to his travel bureau to purchase tickets for a European trip. Examining the files, he discovered that she had bought one round-trip ticket and one one-way ticket. This led him to believe that she never expected Mr. Elkins to return.

THE LOST COIN .... page 46

Paul is the rightful owner of the coin. While a person does not lose his right of ownership merely because he drops something on another person's land, Bill's statement that he dropped this same coin on this same spot four months ago is not convincing. Both he and Dan agree that the coin glitters. But a coin buried beneath the sand for so long would lose its sparkle. Therefore, we may conclude that Bill is lying. As for Sam and Brad, they are mistaken about the law. Seeing or finding something does not in itself confer ownership. Paul is right. He owns the land; therefore, he owns everything on it.

THE ISLAND OF KO .... page 47

If the inhabitant questioned were Red, his second response would have to be "Red." If he were Green, his second response would have to be a lie, "Red." Therefore, he must be a Half-Breed. His second response is therefore a lie, so his first response is true. Tom is the name of the Half-Breed.

Tom's third response must be true. Therefore, Dick is the Red. Obviously, Harry must be the Green.

THE STEEL BEAM .... page 47

The ¾-pound weight is equal to ¼ of a beam. Therefore, the beam must weigh four times ¾ of a pound, or three pounds.

THREE SONS .... page 48

Brown Jr., could not have been the politician (statement 2).

Since Smith, Sr., because of being a paralytic, could not have played golf (statement 4), and since the politician's father played golf (statement 3), Smith, Jr., could not have been the politician.

If neither Brown, Jr., nor Smith, Jr., was the politician, Jones, Jr., must have been he.

Statement 1 tells us that the lawyer frequently played tennis with his father. Because Smith, Sr., could not have played tennis (statement 4), Smith, Jr., could not have been the lawyer. We have previously discovered that he was not the politician. He must, then, have been the banker.

Since Jones, Jr., was the politician and Smith, Jr., was the banker, Brown, Jr., must have been the lawyer.

THE VANISHED COIN .... page 49

The coin which had been inadvertently mislaid was a great rarity. The stranger, being a collector of antiques and coins, happened to have in his vest pocket the only other specimen extant of the coin which Lewis had brought from the Continent. If the stranger submitted to a search of his person, the prize coin would have been found upon him and he would have been accused of stealing it. If he resisted the accusation of theft, his own coin would have been taken from him, since all would have avowed that the coin belonged to Lewis. The stranger did not wish to lose his own valuable coin. The reason that the stranger did not exhibit his own coin to the assembled guests in the first instance was that, since he was an invited guest, it would have been a breach of propriety to steal the show from Lewis, who was a member and inordinately proud of his prize find.

NARROW ESCAPE .... page 50

The fallacy is that Mr. Drake, who must have been looking out the window on the right side of his car to see any possible damage, could not have seen the sun on that side while he was traveling north.

IT REALLY HAPPENED ONE NIGHT page 51

On close consideration of the facts, it is apparent that Winston's objective was to waken Malcolm solely for the purpose of *awakening him*. He never intended to communicate with him. Nor did he.

The only reason that Winston could have for wishing to accomplish his apparent mischief was that Malcolm, by sleeping, was doing *him* a mischief. You see, Winston and Malcolm were both tenants in the same apartment house, and Winston's bedroom adjoined Malcolm's. Malcolm was snoring so loudly that Winston couldn't fall alseep. The victim's only chance, which he cleverly saw, was to disturb the and beat him to the snooze.

THE DORMITORY PUZZLE .... page 52

Room 1—Kim from New York
Room 2—Lisa from Kansas City
Room 3—Tina from Los Angeles
Room 4—Rita from Chicago
Room 5—Mona from Cleveland
Room 6—Ruth from Cincinnati

THE FOOTBALL TOURNAMENT ... page 53

From statement (1), we know that Albie's team made its only score in the final game by a touchdown; from statement (4), the purple team scored only a field goal in this game. Therefore, Albie's team beat the purple team 6-3 in the play-off.

Statement (3) shows that Ben's team survived the first round by defeating Tulane, and must therefore have been the purple team that was defeated by Albie's team in the play-off.

Knowing the above facts, and statements (3) and (6), we can now bracket the teams thus:

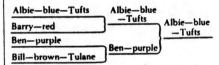

It is now obvious that Bill must have been captain of Tulane.

We see that Tulane was the only team that Albie's team did not meet. Statement (7) proves that Tulane was the brown team.

From statement (2), it is apparent that the red team must have been Barry's and that Albie's team was Tufts.

Since we have found that the red, purple, and brown teams were Barry's, Ben's, and Bill's respectively, Albie's team must have been blue.

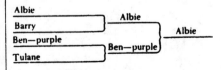

As Trinity did not play Ben's team, the brackets show us that Trinity was Barry's team.

Therefore, Ben's team must have been Temple, and the complete brackets look like this:

GAMESMANSHIP .... page 54

	Bridge	Ten.	Backg.	Check.
Carol	✗	✗	✗	✓
Eloise	✓	✗	✗	✗
Gwen	✗	✗	✓	✗
Joan	✗	✓	✗	✗

For this problem, you might proceed by crossing out the boxes when the clues indicate what the women are *not* experts in. Then you can check the appropriate box as you deduce what each woman excels in. Carol isn't the backgammon champ (clue 3), nor are Eloise or Joan (clue 4), so it's Gwen who excels in backgammon. Gwen, the backgammon whiz, has never played any games with Carol (clue 3), or with Joan (clue 4), so the bridge expert, with whom Gwen *has* played (clue 1), can only be Eloise. We're now left with Carol and Joan, who must be the tennis and checkers experts. But who is which? Clue 2 indicates that Carol isn't the tennis star, so it's Joan for tennis, and Carol for checkers.

THE FORTY-TWO BEERS .... page 55

Who paid for the beers? Why the American, of course! There is no disputing the fact that he paid currency each time he bought a drink. The point is that he increased the value of the currency which he got in return; that is, he increased the 90¢ change he got on each transaction by walking across the border. He added value to the currency by transferring it from one place to another.

There is nothing more startling about this increase in value than there is about buying an object in China that is worth 10¢ there, and transporting it to America where it is worth 50¢. The American who performed the work of carrying a Guatelavian dollar from Tinto to Guatelavia performed 10¢ worth of work from the viewpoint of economics.

COUNT THE TRAINS .... page 56

Thirteen trains. Since it takes six hours to make the trip from Washington to New York, the train which is pulling into New York as Tom's train leaves left Washington at 5 a.m. Tom will arrive in Washington six hours later, or at 5 p.m. He will therefore pass trains which left or will leave Washington at the following hours: 5 a.m.—6 a.m.—7 a.m.—8 a.m.— 9 a.m.—10 a.m.—11 a.m.—12 n.—1 p.m.— 2 p.m. —3 p.m.—4 p.m. Of course, at the exact moment his train pulls into the Washington station, a train will be leaving for New York. If he is alert, he will also see this one. The answer then is 13 trains.

THE HORSE TRADER .... page 57

Twenty-nine horses. This problem is very easy if you work it backwards. The trader had one horse on which to ride home. He disposed of the next to the last horse as a trading fee when he exited from the third fair. This makes a total of two. Since he sold half of his remaining string at the fair, he must have had four in order to have had two left. He paid one to get in. So he must have arrived at the last fair with *five* horses.

He had to give one horse up on leaving the second fair, so he had had six just before leaving. This is half of what he sold, so he must have had 12 before selling. He also had to pay one to enter, so he had 13 on entering the second fair.

He had given one up on leaving the first fair, so he had had 14 just before leaving. This was half of what he sold, so he must have had 28 after paying one as the entrance fee to the first fair. Thus, he started out with 29.

BOOTS .... page 58

Four dollars and a pair of boots. Of the $50 in change that Plaster gave him, Cobblewell gave the customer $4. Presumably, he put the remaining $46 in his cash register. But he then repaid Plaster $50, thus losing $4.

THE LILY POND .... page 59

Twenty days. If the lily doubles its area every day, then on the day before it has covered the entire pond it must have covered an area equal

223

to one-half the area of the pond. It covers the entire pond in 21 days; thus it covers half the pond in 20 days.

AMERICAN HERITAGE .... page 60

1. Let smoke out
2. They were thought to be East Indians
3. They were exchanged when a peace treaty was signed
4. Twelve
5. Ice cream
6. Navaho
7. Sioux
8. Dawes Act
9. Lewis and Clark
10. Bullboat
11. 2½ million
12. John Smith
13. The unsuccessful resistance of the Texans against Mexican leader Santa Anna

WHICH QUIPSTER? .... page 62

1. Mark Twain
2. George Bernard Shaw
3. Oscar Wilde
4. Robert Benchley
5. Mark Twain
6. Ambrose Bierce
7. Ambrose Bierce
8. Robert Benchley
9. George Bernard Shaw
10. Oscar Wilde
11. Robert Benchley
12. George Bernard Shaw
13. Mark Twain
14 . Robert Benchley
15. Oscar Wilde
16. Ambrose Bierce
17. Mark Twain
18. George Bernard Shaw in *Man and Superman*. Oscar Wilde has a similar statement in *Lady Windermeres Fan*
19. Oscar Wilde
20. Ambrose Bierce

NAME THAT CITY .... page 64

1. Paris
2. Moscow
3. Chicago
4. Venice
5. Brooklyn
6. Tokyo
7. Madrid
8. Syracuse
9. Paris
10. St. Louis
11. Philadelphia
12. Paris
13. Hollywood
14. Venice
15. Rome
16. New York
17. Chicago
18. Washington
19. Hong Kong
20. Verona
21. Cincinnati
22. Morocco
23. Las Vegas
24. Frankfort
25. Manhattan
26. Nuremberg
27. Peking
28. Shanghai
29. Berlin
30. Paris

FOR THE LOVE OF MUSIC .... page 66

1. Lute
2. Fiddle
3. Guitar
4. Organ
5. Violin
6. Banjo
7. Bell
8. Harp
9. Guitar
10. Bassoon
11. Fiddle
12. Flute
13. Flute
14. Two drums and a fife
15. Guitar
16. Piano
17. Ram's-horn trumpets
18. Lute
19. Clarinet
20. Zither

COLOR ME! .... page 68

1. Yellow
2. Green
3. Black
4. Gold
5. Scarlet
6. White
7. Black
8. White
9. Red
10. Blue
11. Red
12. Blue
13. Lavendar
14. Blue
15. Black
16. Rose
17. Gold
18. Red
19. Red
20. Gold
21. Gray
22. Gray
23. Green
24. Blue
25. White
26. Blue
27. Black
28. Yellow
29. Red
30. Orange
31. White
32. Amber
33. Brown
34. Scarlet
35. Green

MYSTERY SLEUTHS .... page 70

1. Hercule Poirot   R h
2. Philip Marlowe   M r
3. Father Brown   F p
4. Nero Wolfe   G q
5. C. Auguste Dupin   A e
6. Tabaret   T g
7. Sam Spade   J b
8. 007   S c
9. Tommy Hambledon   N s
10. Sherlock Holmes   B i

11. Perry Mason   H   l
12. Charlie Chan   C   k
13. Lew Archer   O   o
14. Philo Vance   D   n
15. Mike Hammer   Q   f
16. Roderick Alleyn   L   j
17. Peter Wimsey   J   n
18. Dr. Gideon Fell   K   d
19. Ellery Queen   E   a
20. Travis McGee   P   t

CUT AND DRIED .... page 72

In some cases there are two or more possible answers, depending upon the section of the country from which you come. In scoring such divergence from the answers here given, you will of course be as honest as the day is long.

1. Daisy	29. Toast
2. Berry	30. Mouse
3. Pin	31. Gold
4. Whip	32. Kitten, puppy
5. Rain	33. Bat
6. Punch	34. Pig, house
7. Peacock	35. Rail, board
8. Lamb	36. Wolf
9. Lion	37. Doornail
10. Poker, board	38. Whistle
11. Lead	39. Babe
12. Feather	40. Sugar
13. Fiddle	41. Picture
14. Grass	42. Sin
15. Coal, night	43. Mule
16. Sheet	44. Lemon
17. Colt	45. Punch
18. Ghost	46. Judge
19. Lark	47. Dog
20. Pie	48. Crystal
21. Nails	49. Razor
22. Rag	50. Bee
23. Molasses	51. Hen's teeth
24. Flash	52. Turtle
25. Crutch	53. Tack
26. Fox	54. Ocean
27. Ice	55. Day in June
28. Cucumber	56. Penny

SAILORS AND THEIR SHIPS ...... page 74

1. Huckleberry Finn   F   j
   Huckleberry Finn
2. Richard Dana   C   i
   Two Years Before the Mast
3. Fletcher Christian   K   b
   Mutiny on the Bounty
4. Harvey Cheyne   J   g
   Captains Courageous
5. Wolf Larsen & Humphrey Van Weyden   E   d
   The Sea Wolf
6. Horatio Hornblower   H   c
   Captain Horatio Hornblower
7. Philip Francis Queeg   L   f
   The Caine Mutiny
8. Jim Hawkins   B   h
   Treasure Island
9. James Wait   G   l
   Nigger of the Narcissus
10. Ishmael   A   k
    Moby Dick
11. Captain Nemo   I   e
    Twenty Thousand Leagues Under the Sea
12. Santiago   D   a
    The Old Man and the Sea

BY THE NUMBERS .... page 76

1. 14		16. 41
2. 1		17. $\frac{1}{9}$
3. 48		18. 15
4. 56		19. 100
5. 108		20. 206
6. 62		21. 12
7. 2		22. 87
8. 7		23. 11
9. Fahrenheit 451		24. 13
10. 773,692		25. 5
11. 9		26. 90 feet
12. 11		27. 10
13. 1841: Van Buren, William Harrison, Tyler. 1881: Hayes, Garfield, Arthur.		28. 336
		29. 10
		30. 500
		31. 220
		32. 7
14. 10 feet		33. 6
15. 17		34. 27
		35. 969

IN SICKNESS AND IN HEALTH .... page 79

1. *False.* You may cause injury to the delicate nasal tissue. You may try to remove it gently with a finger, but it is best to have a doctor remove it.
2. *False.* The body burns up calories during a fever and should be replenished with light easily- digested foods and juices.
3. *False.* Some mild illnesses produce high fevers, while more severe ones can cause a decline below normal.

225

4. *False.* It is important to determine what caused the pain before any treatment is used. An abdominal pain could indicate appendicitis, and in such a case, heat treatment would be extremely dangerous.
5. *False.* Sickrooms should be kept at a normal temperature (68 to 70 degrees). Old and feeble people, however, may require more heat because of lowered circulation.
6. *False.* Fans will make a patient more comfortable in hot weather, but the flow of air should not be directed on the sick person.
7. *False.* A healthy person's temperature may vary by as much as two degrees on a single day.
8. *False.* Some drugs spoil; some lose their value; some increase in potency. In addition, a drug that is helpful to one patient may be dangerous for another person suffering from the same ailment. Consult your doctor before using anything but the simplest medication.
9. *True.*
10. *False.* Urge him to try to cough it out, or have him bend over and tap him lightly on the upper back. If this doesn't dislodge the bone, see a doctor.
11. *True.*
12. *True.*

FOR BETTE DAVIS FANS .... page 80

1. Ruth Elizabeth Davis
2. Lowell, Massachusetts
3. Martha Graham
4. *Beyond the Forest*
5. George Cukor
6. Somerset Maugham
7. Claude Rains
8. 1938
9. *The Catered Affair*
10. Warner Brothers Studios
11. 1931
12. *Dangerous*
13. Elizabeth I of England
14. Joan Crawford
15. Actor Gary Merrill
16. Margot Channing, in *All About Eve*
17. 1941
18. *Sunset Boulevard.* The star was Gloria Swanson

19. Three. Two of the children are adopted
20. *The Man Who Played God*
21. Humphrey Bogart
22. Universal

REMEMBER RADIO? .... page 82

1. *Our Gal Sunday*
2. *Fibber McGee and Molly*
3. Dashiell Hammett
4. Fay and Evey
5. 39
6. Charles Cantor
7. Jones
8. *The Shadow*
9. Fanny Brice
10. San Francisco
11. Newspaperman
12. *The Maxwell House Showboat*
13. Walter Connolly
14. Chick
15. 640 and 1240 AM
16. Matt Dillon
17. Quiz show
18. Art Linkletter
19. *Hilltop House*
20. Lucky Strike
21. Sam Spade
22. Elmwood
23. The Falcon
24. *The Green Hornet*
25. Gertrude Berg

FREE-FOR-ALL .... page 84

1. *False.* The largest country in the world is the U.S.S.R., at 8,650,000 miles. China is the second largest country, at 3,691,500 miles.
2. *True.*
3. *True.*
4. *False.* A tatterdemalion is a person wearing ragged or tattered clothing.
5. *False.* The most populous country in the world is China. India is the second most populous country.
6. *True.*
7. *False.* Johnny Appleseed's real name was John Chapman. Paul Bunyan was the folk hero of lumber-camp tall tales.
8. *False.* An oxymoron is a figure of speech that combines opposite or contradictory ideas, such as: terribly good, sweet sorrow.
9. *False.* Vivien Leigh played Scarlett O'Hara.
10. *True.*
11. *False.* Tagliatelle is a type of noodles or pasta. Maria Taglioni was the ballerina.
12. *False.* Aaron Burr killed Alexander Hamilton in a duel.

13. *False.* Mali is a country in West Africa.
14. *True.*
15. *False.* A numismatist is a person who collects or studies money and medals. An entomologist studies insects.
16. *True.*
17. *False.* The author of *Volpone* was Shakespeare's contemporary, Ben Jonson.
18. *True.*
19. *True.*
20. *False.* The *New York Gazette*, brought out by William Bradford in 1725, was the first New York newspaper.
21. *False.* Something that is nugatory is worthless.
22. *True,* in 1910.
23. *True.*
24. *True.*
25. *False.* James S. Thurman invented the vacuum cleaner, in 1899. James Thurber (1894–1961) was a popular cartoonist and writer.
26. *False.* A griffin doesn't exist anywhere. It is a mythical animal with the body of a lion and the head of an eagle.
27. *True.*
28. *True.*
29. *False.* Escudos are Portuguese coins. The monetary unit of Peru is the sol.
30. *False.* It is 6:00 P.M. in Cairo, or six hours later than New York.
31. *False.* The capital of California is Sacramento.
32. *False.* It was signed by King John in 1215. The Normans, under William the Conqueror, defeated the Saxons at the Battle of Hastings in 1066.
33. *True.*
34. *True.*
35. *False. All About Eve* was directed by Joseph Mankiewicz.

HOOP-LA! .... page 86

1. Rhode Island State
2. Wilt Chamberlain, with a total of 31,419 points scored
3. James Naismith
4. Ferdinand Lewis Alcindor
5. Boston Celtics
6. 75,000

7. Mu Tieh-Chu who was 7' 9.75" tall
8. Nat Holman, also known as Mr. Basketball
9. 20,000
10. Canada, in 1893
11. Third
12. New York City College, in 1949–1950
13. The Stilt
14. 1890s
15. 22
16. Oscar Robertson, who sank a total of 7,694 free throws in his career with the Cincinatti Royals and Milwaukee Bucks
17. Interference with the ball on its final arch toward the basket
18. Wesleyan and Yale
19. 12
20. 1936
21. Run holding the ball
22. 100, by Wilt Chamberlain
23. 24 seconds
24. .275
25. United States
26. Bill Walton
27. Indiana
28. John Havlicek, who played 1,270 games for the Boston Celtics
29. Bill Russell
30. U.S.S.R.
31. Center
32. $20,000

COMMON COGNOMENS .... page 89

1. Smith	6. Miller
2. Johnson	7. Davis
3. Williams	8. Anderson
4. Jones	9. Wilson
5. Brown	10. Thompson

GRAB BAG .... page 90

1. A person of low intelligence
2. Lhasa, Tibet, at an elevation of 12,002 feet
3. Alexander Pope
4. Deer
5. Guinea, Africa, with an average life expectancy of 27 years
6. Musical instrument which resembles a xylophone

7. Timbuktu Mali, where the average temperature is 84.7° F
8. Reversion to characteristics in one's remote ancestors
9. Bette Davis
10. Gigantic, after Swift's land of giants in *Gulliver's Travels*
11. A quadrilateral rectangle having only two sides parallel
12. Walt Whitman
13. Goldsmith Maid
14. Eatables
15. 29.7 mph
16. The British Museum
17. Giuseppe Verdi
18. Golfer
19. Australia
20. Matthew Webb
21. Bees
22. New Jersey
23. Earth

ACO . . . . page 93

1. Acolyte
2. Aconite
3. Acorn
4. Acoustic
5. Anacoluthon
6. Anaconda
7. Bacon
8. Beacon
9. Cacography
10. Cacodyl
11. Cacophony
12. Catacomb
13. Deacon
14. Laconic
15. Placoid
16. Raconteur
17. Seacoast
18. Taco

ARN . . . . page 93

1. Arnica
2. Barn
3. Barnyard
4. Barnacle
5. Carnage
6. Carnal
7. Carnival
8. Carnivorous
9. Charnelhouse
10. Darn
11. Earn
12. Earnest
13. Garner
14. Garnet
15. Garnish
16. Harness
17. Learn
18. Nearness
19. Tarn
20. Tarnation
21. Tarnish
22. Varnish
23. Warn
24. Yarn
25. Yearn

NCO . . . . page 94

1. Banco
2. Bunco
3. Buncombe
4. Encode
5. Encoil
6. Encompass
7. Incognito
8. Incoherent
9. Income
10. Incommode
11. Incommunicado
12. Incompatibility
13. Incompetent
14. Incomplete
15. Incomprehensible
16. Inconceivable
17. Inconclusive
18. Incongruent
19. Inconsequential
20. Inconsistent
21. Inconspicuous
22. Inconstant
23. Incontinent
24. Inconvenience
25. Incorporate
26. Incorrect
27. Incorrigible
28. Nincompoop
29. Noncombatant
30. Noncombustible
31. Noncomissioned
32. Uncoil
33. Uncollar
34. Uncollected
35. Uncomfortable
36. Uncommon
37. Uncommunicative
38. Unconcerned
39. Unconditional
40. Unconnected
41. Unconscious
42. Uncontaminated
43. Uncontrolled
44. Unconventional
45. Uncooked
46. Uncooperative
47. Uncoordinated
48. Uncork
49. Uncorrected
50. Uncountable
51. Uncouple
52. Uncouth
53. Uncover

EPT .... **page 99**

1. Accept
2. Adept
3. Concept
4. Crept
5. Deceptive
6. Except
7. Inception
8. Intercept
9. Inept
10. Kleptomania
11. Misconception
12. Peptic
13. Peptone
14. Perception
15. Precept
16. Receptacle
17. Reception
18. Receptive
19. Reptile
20. Sceptre
21. Septennial
22. Septic
23. Septuagenarian
24. Septum
25. Skeptical
26. Slept
27. Streptococcus
28. Swept
29. Transept
30. Wept

LBO .... **page 99**

1. Bellbird
2. Bellboy
3. Bilbo
4. Billboard
5. Callbox
6. Callboy
7. Elbow
8. Hellbox
9. Sailboard
10. Sailboat
11. Shellback
12. Spellbound

AGO .... **page 100**

1. Agony
2. Agoraphobia
3. Agouti
4. Anagoge
5. Antagonist
6. Decagon
7. Demagogue
8. Diagonal
9. Dodecagon
10. Dragoman
11. Dragon
12. Dragonnade
13. Dragoon
14. Farrago
15. Flagon
16. Heptagon
17. Hexagon
18. Imago
19. Lagoon
20. Nonagon
21. Octagon
22. Pagoda
23. Paragon
24. Pedagogy
25. Pentagon
26. Phagocyte
27. Protagonist
28. Ragout
29. Sago
30. Wagon

RDU .... **page 100**

1. Arduous
2. Corduroy
3. Overdue
4. Perdurable
5. Stardust
6. Verdure

HLO .... **page 101**

1. Chlorine
2. Chloroform
3. Chlorophyl
4. Decathlon
5. Hydrochloric
6. Matchlock
7. Pentathlon
8. Phlox

RLO .... **page 102**

1. Airlock
2. Carload
3. Charlock
4. Charlotte
5. Earlobe
6. Earlock
7. Forlorn
8. Furlong
9. Furlough
10. Harlot
11. Interlock
12. Interlocution
13. Interlope
14. Merlon
15. Orlon
16. Overload
17. Overlong
18. Overlook
19. Overlord
20. Parlor
21. Parlous
22. Purloin
23. Sugarloaf
24. Warlock
25. Warlord

FTY .... **page 102**

1. Crafty
2. Drafty
3. Fifty
4. Hefty
5. Lofty
6. Nifty
7. Shifty
8. Softy
9. Swifty

LTR .... **page 103**

1. Altruism
2. Caltrop
3. Cultrate
4. Filtration
5. Infiltrate
6. Paltry
7. Philtre
8. Poltroon
9. Poultry
10. Sultry
11. Ultrasonic
12. Ultraviolet

ABA .... **page 103**

1. Aback
2. Abacus
3. Abalone
4. Abandon
5. Abase
6. Abash
7. Abate
8. Abatis
9. Abattoir
10. Alabaster
11. Anabas
12. Anabatic
13. Cabal
14. Caballine
15. Cabana
16. Cabane
17. Cabaret
18. Calabash
19. Cinnabar
20. Fleabag
21. Fleabane
22. Garbardine
23. Labarum
24. Seabag

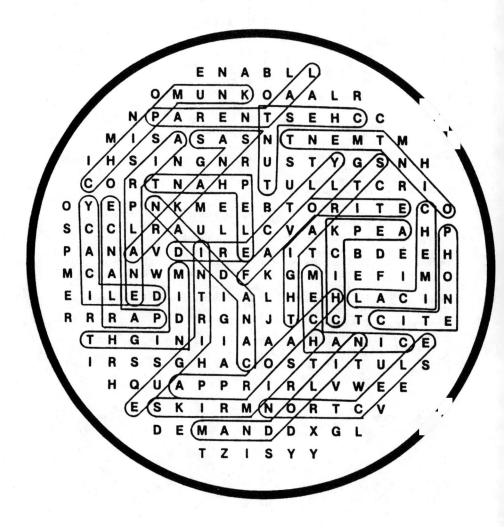

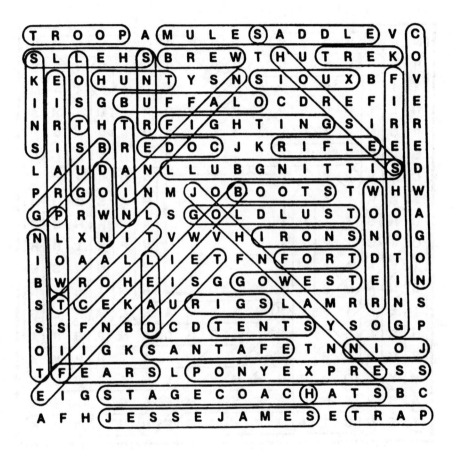

233

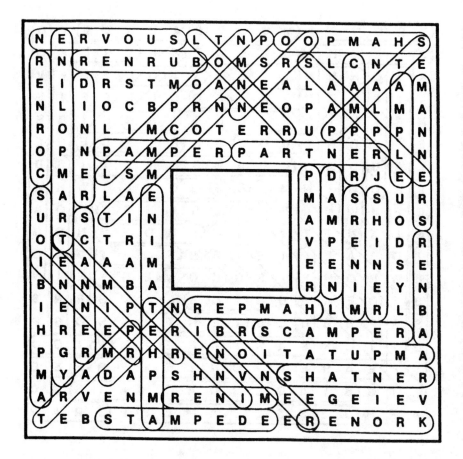

234

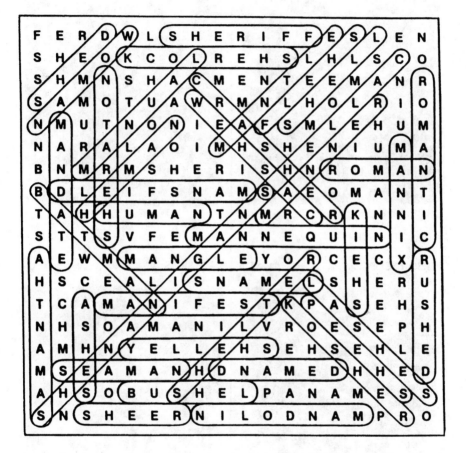

235

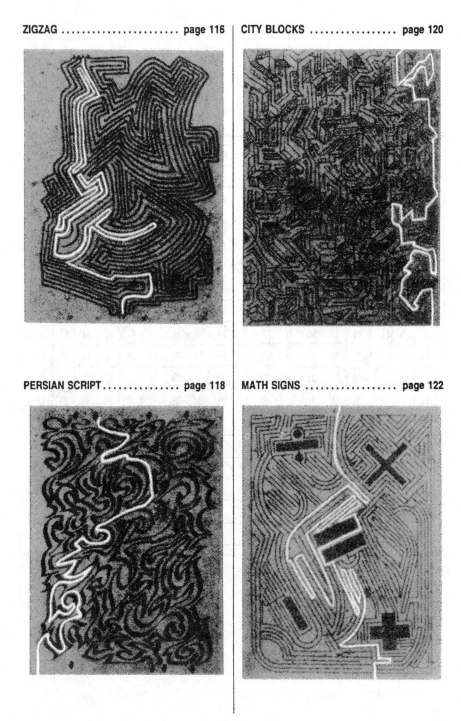

236

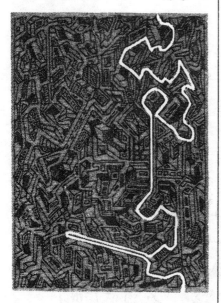

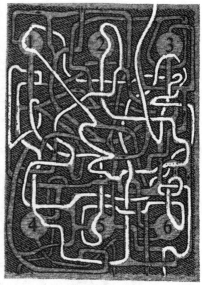

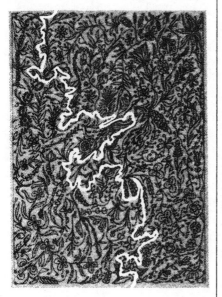

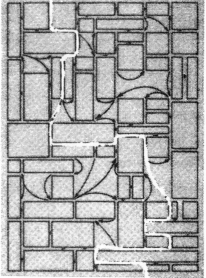

CROSSWORD PUZZLE NO. 1 . . . . . page 136

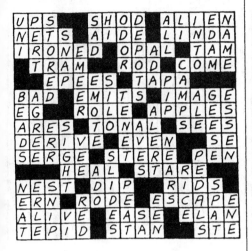

CROSSWORD PUZZLE NO. 3 . . . . page 140

CROSSWORD PUZZLE NO. 2 . . . . . page 138

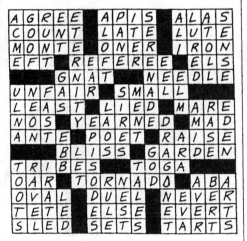

CROSSWORD PUZZLE NO. 4 . . . . page 142

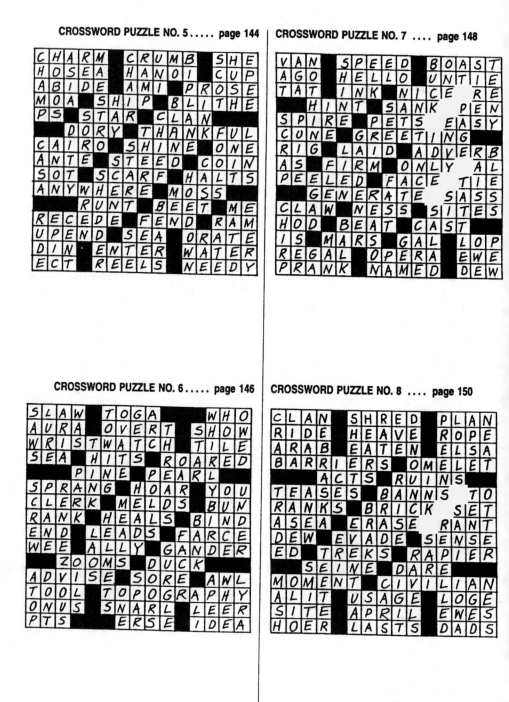

CROSSWORD PUZZLE NO. 5

```
C H A R M   C R U M B   S H E
H O S E A   H A N O I   C U P
A B I D E   A M I   P R O S E
M O A   S H I P   B L I T H E
P S   S T A R   C L A N
    D O R Y   T H A N K F U L
C A I R O   S H I N E   O N E
A N T E   S T E E D   C O I N
S O T   S C A R F   H A L T S
A N Y W H E R E   M O S S
    R U N T   B E E T   M E
R E C E D E   F E N D   R A M
U P E N D   S E A   O R A T E
D I N   E N T E R   W A T E R
E C T   R E E L S   N E E D Y
```

CROSSWORD PUZZLE NO. 7

```
V A N   S P E E D   B O A S T
A G O   H E L L O   U N T I E
T A T   I N K   N I C E   R E
    H I N T   S A N K   P E N
S P I R E   P E T S   E A S Y
C O N E   G R E E T I N G
R I G   L A I D   A D V E R B
A S   F I R M   O N L Y   A L
P E E L E D   F A C E   T I E
    G E N E R A T E   S A S S
C L A W   N E S S   S I T E S
H O D   B E A T   C A S T
I S   M A R S   G A L   L O P
R E G A L   O P E R A   E W E
P R A N K   N A M E D   D E W
```

CROSSWORD PUZZLE NO. 6

```
S L A W   T O G A   W H O
A U R A   O V E R T   S H O W
W R I S T W A T C H   T I L E
S E A   H I T S   R O A R E D
    P I N E   P E A R L
S P R A N G   H O A R   Y O U
C L E R K   M E L D S   B U N
R A N K   H E A L S   B I N D
E N D   L E A D S   F A R C E
W E E   A L L Y   G A N D E R
    Z O O M S   D U C K
A D V I S E   S O R E   A W L
T O O L   T O P O G R A P H Y
O N U S   S N A R L   L E E R
P T S   E R S E   I D E A
```

CROSSWORD PUZZLE NO. 8

```
C L A N   S H R E D   P L A N
R I D E   H E A V E   R O P E
A R A B   E A T E N   E L S A
B A R R I E R S   O M E L E T
    A C T S   R U I N S
T E A S E S   B A N N S   T O
R A N K S   B R I C K   S E T
A S E A   E R A S E   R A N T
D E W   E V A D E   S E N S E
E D   T R E K S   R A P I E R
    S E I N E   D A R E
M O M E N T   C I V I L I A N
A L I T   U S A G E   L O G E
S I T E   A P R I L   E W E S
H O E R   L A S T S   D A D S
```

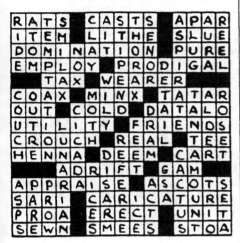 

CROSSWORD PUZZLE NO. 9 — page 152

R	A	T	S		C	A	S	T	S		A	P	A	R
I	T	E	M		L	I	T	H	E		S	L	U	E
D	O	M	I	N	A	T	I	O	N		P	U	R	E
E	M	P	L	O	Y		P	R	O	D	I	G	A	L
	T	A	X		W	E	A	R	E	R				
C	O	A	X		M	I	N	X		T	A	T	A	R
O	U	T		C	O	L	D		D	A	T	A	L	O
U	T	I	L	I	T	Y		F	R	I	E	N	D	S
C	R	O	U	C	H		R	E	A	L		T	E	E
H	E	N	N	A		D	E	E	M		C	A	R	T
		A	D	R	I	F	T		G	A	M			
A	P	P	R	A	I	S	E		A	S	C	O	T	S
S	A	R	I		C	A	R	I	C	A	T	U	R	E
P	R	O	A		E	R	E	C	T		U	N	I	T
S	E	W	N		S	M	E	E	S		S	T	O	A

CROSSWORD PUZZLE NO. 11 — page 156

B	A	S	E	B	A	L	L		S	E	A	S	O	N
A	N	I	M	A	L	I	A		M	A	N	T	L	E
B	I	D	E	N	T		M	E	A	S	U	R	E	S
B	L	I	N	K		M	E	R	L	E		E	A	T
L	I	N	D		F	I	N	A	L		C	A	R	L
E	N	G		P	A	N	T	S		R	A	M	I	E
R	E		C	O	R	E	S		A	E	N	E	A	S
		T	R	I	E	S		L	E	V	E	R		
S	E	R	I	N	S		D	E	T	E	R		S	O
A	L	I	S	T		M	E	T	A	L		F	E	N
L	U	M	P		S	E	C	T	S		L	U	C	E
U	S	E		E	W	E	R	S		B	A	T	O	N
T	I	T	I	V	A	T	E		D	I	V	I	N	E
E	V	E	N	E	R		E	M	E	R	A	L	D	S
R	E	R	E	A	D		S	E	E	D	L	E	S	S

CROSSWORD PUZZLE NO. 10 — page 154

C	H	O	P		S	I	S	A	L		Q	U	A	D
L	I	R	A		I	R	A	T	E		U	R	G	E
A	V	E	R		B	O	N	E		S	E	N	N	A
Y	E	A	R	L	I	N	G		F	O	S	S	I	L
		D	O	I	L	Y		C	O	A	T			
F	M		T	E	A		M	A	R	R	I	A	G	E
J	A	R		S	N	E	E	R		S	O	B	E	R
E	L	A	M		T	A	T	A	R		N	E	N	E
C	A	N	O	E		S	E	T	O	N		T	I	C
T	R	A	N	S	F	E	R		Y	E	T		I	T
		S	T	U	D		D	A	V	I	T			
S	K	A	T	E	R		D	E	L	E	T	I	O	N
L	I	N	E	R		L	O	T	I		L	A	D	E
E	W	E	R		R	A	Z	E	S		E	R	O	S
W	I	T	S		E	X	E	R	T		D	A	R	T

CROSSWORD PUZZLE NO. 12 — page 158

S	H	O	P		C	H	E	A	P		R	O	A	R
T	O	R	E		H	I	N	G	E		E	D	G	E
O	M	A	R		A	D	D	E	D		F	O	R	A
W	E	L	F	A	R	E		N	A	T	U	R	A	L
			I	L	L		A	T	L	A	S			
H	E	A	D	L	A	N	D	S		R	A	G	E	D
A	L	L	Y			T	E	D		C	O	L	L	A	R
R	A	T		P	A	T	R	I	O	T		E	R	E
S	T	A	M	E	N		E	R	R		G	A	L	A
H	E	R	O	N		P	S	E	U	D	O	N	Y	M
		C	A	N	I	S		S	O	L				
H	A	C	K	L	E	S		S	C	R	I	B	E	S
A	B	L	E		S	T	O	L	A		A	L	T	O
T	E	A	R		T	I	B	E	T		T	U	N	A
E	D	D	Y		S	L	I	D	E		H	E	A	P

```
C H A R M S . . . C H I P I N
R O S E A T E . C R U S A D E
O P I A T E S . R E T I L E S
W E A L . A T L A S . S E A T
. . . R E E F S . . . . . . .
E E L S . I R A T E . H A T S
S T A M E N S . S T H E N I A
T A M E R . . . . A L I G N .
O P A L I N E . D A P P L E D
P E S T . E N T E R . S E R S
. . . O L I V E . . . . . . .
A H A B . L A P I N . A D A M
G E N E T I C . S O I L A G E
E M A N A T E . E S T A T E S
S P L A S H . . . E S S E D A
```

```
C O M F O R T A B L E . P A S S I V E
O . A . D . A . L . L . A . L . N . G
M U S E D . I R A T E L Y . O C C U R
E . T . M . L . Z . C . M . V . L . E
T H E R E F O R E . T H E R A P I S T
. R . N . R . . . O . N . K . N . . .
R E P U T E . S E C R E T S . M E S S
E . I . S P A N . . S A P . . . . . A
P E E L . I R K S O M E . M I N C E D
E . C . A C T . U . I . H I P . O . I
A V E N G E . B E A G L E S . I M P S
L . . E N D . . H . W E D . . P . T
S U D S . E R U D I T E . N O B L E S
. R . S . I . E . . . B . U . A . . .
C H A N C E F U L . S H A M B L I N G
L . G . A . T . U . E . R . T . N . I
I N N E R . E N G I N E D . F I L I N G
M . E . C . R . E . N . I . U . N . O
B O T H E R S . S E A R C H L I G H T
```

```
C O S T . S P A T . S A T A N
A W A Y . P O R E . I R E N E
B L U R . A R R E S T M E N T
. . T A B . R A P E S . M E T
S C E N E . I N E Z . V E A L
C A R T R I D G E . S I D L E
A N N . E D G E . D E E . . .
N E E . A L E . P I E . C H A
. . I V Y . B A S T . R A P
S P I C E . K E R C H I E F S
L A D Y . P I C T . E N A T E
I R E . M E R L E . S U M .
G L A D I A T O R S . R E A L
H O T E L . L U R E . E R N E
T R E N D . E D E N . D Y A D
```

```
S T A R T S . S T A L L S
T I C K E T . P A N O U T
O M I O . R O E . T U B E
P E D . B U N C O . T E T
. . . C U T . I N F . . .
F O U R S . P A T R I C K
E I N E . T I L . E V O E
B L O W O U T . P O E S Y
. . S A N . T I N . . . .
M A P . S E V E N . P R E
A B O U . U A R . L E O S
R U N S U P . S P A R K S
S T E E R S . E X C U S E
```

The past is always picturesque. Distance lends enchantment, for it covers the greasy spots on His Majesty's plumed hat with a charitable layer of dust.

Van Loon
The Story of America

The penitentiary was intended to lead the convicted to penitence. What is too frequently overlooked is that prisons generate far more anger than remorse.

Arthur Lelyveld
Punishment: For and Against

If you have wit, use it please and not to hurt. You may shine like the sun in the temperate zones, without scorching.

Lord Chesterfield

Pensive plodding impecunious portrait painter seeks solemn spinsterish subjects for visual study.

Please recall just when you last consumed sufficient kohlrabi. This most important question evidences how cryptography can drive one mad.

The streets of Sydney were already filled with detribalized natives, some stark naked. The prodigious buck would create no interest in the Australian born lass. The newly arrived could be instantly discerned by her maidenly blushes.

Harris and Forbes
The Land That Waited

Vodka rivals arak when vitriolic liquors vie for honors. Likewise ptarmigan rivals venison when gourmets evaluate piquant viands.

A friend may well be reckoned the masterpiece of nature.

Ralph Waldo Emerson

Nothing except a battle lost can be half so melancholy as a battle won.

Duke of Wellington

Thanks for any fun the gal had was not due him nor his gay mad act. Shy but sly, she won joy via gin.

There comes a time in life, my dear Blubber, when we must take the bull by the tail and face the situation.

W. C. Fields

They that can give up essential liberty to obtain a little temporary safety deserve neither liberty nor safety.

Benjamin Franklin

He that hath wife and children hath given hostages to fortune; for they are impediments to great enterprises either of virtue or of mischief.

Francis Bacon

1. Bugle
2. French horn
3. Lyre
4. Lute
5. Ocarina
6. Guitar
7. Fife
8. Cymbals
9. Buccina
10. Bassoon
11. Sistrum
12. Trombone
13. Kalimba

SHEPHERD .... page 184

1. Deep	7. Peer	13. Sheep
2. Deer	8. Reed	14. Sheer
3. Heed	9. Seed	15. Sherd
4. Herd	10. Seep	16. Shred
5. Here	11. Seer	17. Speed
6. Hers	12. Shed	18. Sphere

ANTHRACITE .... page 185

1. Anther	14. Enrich	26. Their
2. Antic	15. Heart	27. Thrice
3. Attar	16. Inter	28. Tithe
4. Canter	17. Ranch	29. Trace
5. Cater	18. Rattan	30. Tract
6. Chain	19. Reach	31. Train
7. Chair	20. React	32. Trait
8. Chant	21. Recant	33. Trance
9. Chart	22. Tacit	34. Treat
10. Cheat	23. Teach	35. Trench
11. Crane	24. Tenth	36. Trice
12. Crate	25. Thane	37. Trite
13. Earth		

CHIMERA .... page 186

1. Ache	13. Cream	26. Marc
2. Acme	14. Crime	27. March
3. Acre	15. Each	28. Mare
4. Amice	16. Emir	29. Mica
5. Arch	17. Hair	30. Mice
6. Came	18. Hame	31. Mire
7. Care	19. Hare	32. Race
8. Chair	20. Harem	33. Reach
9. Char	21. Harm	34. Ream
10. Charm	22. Hear	35. Rice
11. Chime	23. Heir	36. Rich
12. Cram	24. Hire	37. Rime
	25. Mace	

REPULSE .... page 186

1. Peruse	4. Purse	6. Rupee
2. Pulse	5. Repel	7. Sleep
3. Puree		8. Slurp

CLAIRVOYANT .... page 187

1. Acorn	20. Coati	39. Rayon
2. Action	21. Coral	40. Rival
3. Actor	22. Corny	41. Royal
4. Antic	23. Crayon	42. Talon
5. Aorta	24. Crony	43. Tonal
6. Atonal	25. Inlay	44. Tonic
7. Avail	26. Irony	45. Trail
8. Canal	27. Ivory	46. Train
9. Cantor	28. Lariat	47. Train
10. Carat	29. Lavatory	48. Vainly
11. Carnal	30. Natal	49. Valor
12. Carnival	31. Naval	50. Vanity
13. Carol	32. Ocarina	51. Variant
14. Carton	33. Ovary	52. Vicar
15. Caviar	34. Racial	53. Victor
16. Cavil	35. Rainy	54. Victory
17. Cavity	36. Ratio	55. Vinyl
18. Cavort	37. Ration	56. Viola
19. Clarion	38. Rational	57. Vital

AMERICAN .... page 188

1. Amen	13. Icer	25. Mine
2. Arcane	14. Mace	26. Mire
3. Area	15. Main	27. Name
4. Aria	16. Mane	28. Near
5. Came	17. Mania	29. Nice
6. Cane	18. Manic	30. Race
7. Care	19. Mare	31. Rain
8. Cram	20. Marine	32. Ream
9. Crane	21. Mean	33. Rein
10. Cream	22. Mice	34. Remain
11. Crime	23. Mien	35. Rice
12. Emir	24. Mince	36. Rime

RECREATIONAL .... page 189

1. Actor	12. Creation	23. Recoil
2. Alien	13. Creel	24. Rental
3. Antic	14. Enter	25. Toiler
4. Antler	15. Loiter	26. Toner
5. Careen	16. Loner	27. Trace
6. Carton	17. Oiler	28. Trail
7. Cater	18. Ration	29. Train
8. Clear	19. Rational	30. Trance
9. Crane	20. React	31. Treacle
10. Crate	21. Reactor	32. Trial
11. Create	22. Recant	33. Trice

246

1. Right
2. Right
3. Wrong
   javelin
4. Right
5. Right
6. Wrong
   siege
7. Wrong
   curriculum
8. Right
9. Right
10. Wrong
    myrrh
11. Wrong
    frankincense
12. Wrong
    inveigle
13. Right
14. Right
15. Wrong
    abhorrent
16. Wrong
    acoustics
17. Wrong
    acumen
18. Right
19. Right
20. Wrong
    iridescent
21. Right
22. Right
23. Right
24. Wrong
    battalion
25. Right
26. Right
27. Right
28. Wrong
    heliotrope
29. Right
30. Wrong
    forcemeat
31. Right
32. Right
33. Wrong
    finesse
34. Wrong
    garrulous
35. Wrong
    sarcophagus
36. Right
37. Wrong
    catastrophes
38. Right
39. Wrong
    pharaoh
40. Right
41. Right
42. Right

43. Wrong	48. Wrong
pomade	_bronchitis_
44. Right	49. Wrong
45. Right	_Doberman_
46. Wrong	_pinscher_
vilify	50. Wrong
47. Right	_sarsaparilla_

HOW CREATIVE ARE YOU? . . . . . . page 214

Give yourself the points indicated for each answer. Then add up your total score.

1. a-6, b-2, c-4	11. a-4, b-2, c-6
2. a-2, b-6, c-4	12. a-2, b-2, c-6
3. a-6, b-2, c-4	13. a-2, b-4, c-6
4. a-2, b-6, c-4	14. a-2, b-6, c-4
5. a-2, b-6, c-6	15. a-2, b-6, c-4
6. a-2, b-4, c-6	16. a-6, b-4, c-2
7. a-6, b-4, c-2	17. a-2, b-6, c-4
8. a-4, b-6, c-2	
9. a-6, b-2, c-6	
10. a-4, b-2, c-6	

IF YOU SCORED:

100 and over: You are a highly creative person on several different levels—a person who is able to see and to act inventively. You are capable of improvising—the sort of person who, lacking a hammer, will drive a nail with a shoe.

80–98: Your score is very good. You are capable of being creative at some levels. Albert Einstein, a mathematical creative genius, said that if he were to return to earth after death, he'd like to be a plumber in his next life because he couldn't fit pipes together properly before.

58–78: You are very likely one of those who would rather not have to think about being creative—a "let-George-do-it" type. However, in all probability, you have one or more jobs or hobbies which spark your creative talents, such as cooking, gardening, painting, and you are probably creative without knowing it.

38–56: Creativity is not your strong point. You're not one of those who can make something out of nothing. Better learn to read manuals carefully and follow directions with accuracy. You are probably a cautious person and will never get into trouble with unwise experimentation.